W9-BOB-015

MORE THAN PETTICOATS

Remarkable Vermont Women

Deborah Clifford

Guilford, Connecticut

Text design by Nancy Freeborn
Map by Daniel Lloyd © 2009 Morris Book Publishing, LLC

Library of Congress Cataloging-in-Publication Data
Clifford, Deborah Pickman.
  More than petticoats. Remarkable Vermont women / Deborah Clifford.
     p. cm. -- (More than petticoats series)
  Includes bibliographical references.
  ISBN 978-0-7627-4306-3
  1. Women--Vermont--Biography. 2. Vermont--Biography. I. Title. II. Title:
Remarkable Vermont women.
  CT3262.V4C55 2009
  920.7209743--dc22
                                        2008042751

Printed in the United States of America
10 9 8 7 6 5 4 3 2 1

CONTENTS

Acknowledgments vii

Introduction ix

Lucy Terry Prince: *Poet and Pioneer* 1

Ann Story: *Pioneer and Patriot* 10

Emma Willard: *Educating Women for the Republic* 18

Clarina Howard Nichols: *A Womanly Reformer* 28

Julia Caroline Ripley Dorr: *A Vermont Poet Laureate* . . . 39

Abby Maria Hemenway:
   The Woman Who Saved Vermont's History 52

Rachael Robinson Elmer: *Independent Artist* 63

Dorothy Canfield Fisher: *Novelist and Crusader* 74

Electra Havemeyer Webb: *Born to Collect* 83

Helen Hartness Flanders:
   Green Mountain Ballad Collector 94

Consuelo Northrop Bailey: *Vermont's Own Daughter* . . . 106

Shirley Jackson:
   Raising Demons in the Green Mountains 116

Selected References 129

About the Author 139

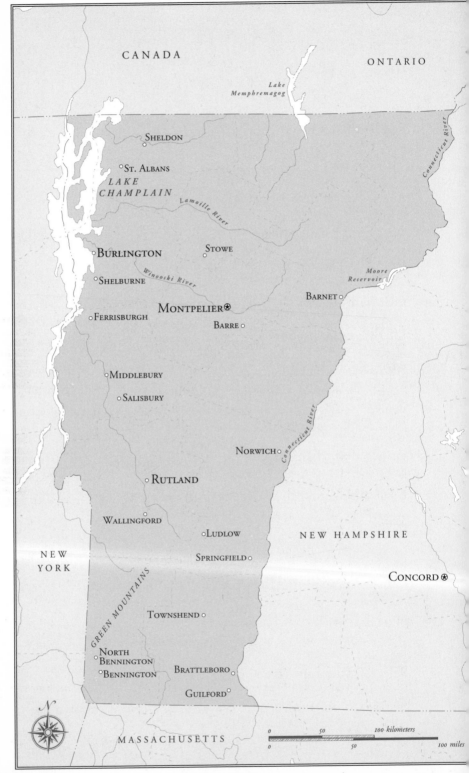

CANADA

ONTARIO

Lake Memphremagog

SHELDON

°ST. ALBANS

LAKE CHAMPLAIN

Lamoille River

Connecticut River

STOWE

BURLINGTON

Winooski River

SHELBURNE

Moore Reservoir

BARNET

MONTPELIER ✪

FERRISBURGH

BARRE

MIDDLEBURY

SALISBURY

NORWICH

Connecticut River

RUTLAND

WALLINGFORD

LUDLOW

NEW HAMPSHIRE

SPRINGFIELD

NEW YORK

CONCORD ✪

GREEN MOUNTAINS

TOWNSHEND

NORTH BENNINGTON

BENNINGTON

BRATTLEBORO

GUILFORD

0   50   100 *kilometers*
0   50   100 miles

MASSACHUSETTS

VERMONT

ACKNOWLEDGMENTS

As this book follows many decades of experience researching and writing about Vermont women, particularly nineteenth-century women, most of those who assisted me in this project are old friends. Shelburne Museum archivist, Polly Darnell, for example, who led me to research materials on Electra Havemeyer Webb—including the photograph of her—is someone I've known and talked about history with since the 1970s. Lyn Blackwell is another friend and scholar who shares my interest in nineteenth-century women reformers and has been a most helpful critic of my writings on Vermont women.

Many other people gave generously of their time in helping me to find both published and unpublished sources. First among these is Andrew Wentinck, curator of Special Collections and Archives at Middlebury College, who, together with his assistant curator, Danielle Rougeau, went out of the way to find materials on many of the women in this collection, including Julia Ripley Dorr, Helen Hartness Flanders, and Emma Willard. Jane Williamson, director of the Rokeby Museum, and her assistant, Jennifer Staats, both helped me get acquainted with the family of Rachael Robinson Elmer and introduced me to Laura Daudelin, who loaned me a draft of a paper she was writing on this Quaker artist. Much of my research on Elmer was done at the Jessica Stewart Swift Library of the Henry Sheldon Museum in Middlebury, where many of the Robinson family papers are stored, and I have both Jane Ploughman and her successor as librarian, Orson Kingsley, to thank for helping with my research there. A long-time volunteer at the Sheldon, Barbara Wells, loaned me some invaluable materials on Julia Dorr, including an unpublished paper by Janice B. Edwards. Finally, Jane Beck, Vermont State Folklorist Emeritus, guided me to an unpublished draft of a novel on Lucy Terry Prince by Mildred Walker, a long-time resident of Guilford.

For help in finding photographs and other images of the women included in this book, I would like to thank a number of people, besides those mentioned above. These include David Hemenway of Shelburne, Vermont; librarian Paul Carnahan and assistant librarian Marjorie Strong at the Vermont Historical Society in Barre; Prudence Doherty of Special Collections, Bailey/Howe Library, University of Vermont; Julie Sopher, Rights and Reproductions manager of the Shelburne Museum; Brian Lindner, corporate historian of the National Life Group; and Laurence Hyman, who kindly supplied a photo of his mother, Shirley Jackson.

Above all, the person to whom I owe the most heartfelt thanks is my husband of fifty-one years, Nicholas R. Clifford. For the last two of those years, this retired professor of history at Middlebury College has not only listened willingly to endless accounts of the dozen women included in this collection, he has also coped patiently with my computer incompetence. Most important, however, he has been my editor-in-chief extraordinaire, even going so far as to read every chapter aloud to me before it was submitted.

INTRODUCTION

There's an old saying that people have been Vermont's greatest export. The famous Illinois Democrat Stephen Douglas, a native of Brandon, echoed this when he claimed back in 1851 that Vermont "was a good state to be born in provided one migrated early." Only one of the women in this book, however, fits Douglas's description: Rachael Robinson Elmer, born in Ferrisburgh and educated in Vermont, made her brief but successful career as an artist in New York City. By contrast, of the eleven others whose lives are featured in this book, seven were actually born outside Vermont, but all made important contributions to its history and culture.

In choosing the women to be included in this collection, I took various criteria into account. First, each must be distinctive in her own right (Grace Coolidge, Vermont's only First Lady, is not found here). Second, taken together, they should represent varied fields of accomplishment. Finally, sufficient resources must exist to provide a rounded picture of each woman's life. When preparing to write this book, I initially chose a number of outstanding Vermont women who later had to be put aside for lack of accessible material documenting their lives, if not their accomplishments. Sad to say, while Vermonters have long expressed a great love for their history, they have been noteworthy in their failure to save its sources. This negligence is especially evident when it comes to unearthing information on women.

If finding sufficient material documenting the lives of these mostly Anglo-Saxon Protestant women is challenging, tracing the lives of women of different races and ethnicities in Vermont is even more difficult. Here, Lucy Prince, a black poet and pioneer, is the single representative of Vermont's racial diversity. This, despite the fact that Native Americans and French Canadians have at various periods in Vermont's history lived here in large numbers. Available information on many who emigrated here is hard to come by, and information on their women is meager at best. This, of course, reflects Vermont's own self-image as a quintessentially Yankee state.

Furthermore, while most of these individuals reflect an idealistic view of Vermont, this state has never been the rural paradise that many people have imagined it to be. Following a settlement boom in the late eighteenth and early nineteenth centuries, its population growth essentially stagnated, as emigrants sought their fortunes in the burgeoning cities of New York and southern New England, as well as the lands opening in the West. Partly because of this, Vermont has been, for most of its history, a poor state and one that has its share of parochialism and inwardness. Yet only two of the portraits included here reflect this darker side, the first and the last: Lucy Terry Prince and Shirley Jackson.

My own interest in Vermont women dates back to the mid-1970s when I was at work on a biography of Julia Ward Howe, author of the "Battle Hymn of the Republic" and an ardent supporter of women's suffrage. I wrote about her 1870 tour of Vermont to promote a suffrage amendment to the state constitution.

Thus, the task of writing brief biographies of twelve notable Vermont women seemed an appropriate one for me to undertake. And, while I've been rewarded by getting to know some old friends better, including Clarina Howard Nichols, Emma Willard, and Consuelo Northrop Bailey, I've derived the greatest pleasure from befriending many others about whom I earlier knew little or nothing. I'm glad to have met them, and I hope you will be too.

LUCY TERRY PRINCE

ca. 1730–1824

Poet and Pioneer

Lucy Terry Prince and her husband Abijah had been waging war with their Guilford neighbor, John Noyes, ever since the late 1770s. Noyes, a recent settler from Connecticut, wanted the Princes' land, which he considered superior to his own, and would go to any lengths to get it. Noyes also disliked having a black couple and their six children as his nearest neighbors.

What Noyes hadn't reckoned with was the Princes' tenacity. They fought every provocation—from destruction of property to outright assaults—by taking John Noyes to court. In the early years it was Abijah (known as Bijah), who defended his rights before the local judge or magistrate, taking Lucy and their two eldest sons along to act as witnesses. Yet, while Bijah enjoyed a string of successes in court, that did not end the harassment.

It was in the spring of 1785 that Noyes's brother Amos broke through the Princes' gate and set about destroying their newly planted crops. The black family now faced total destitution. This time, however, instead of bringing their case to the local court, the Princes, acting on the advice of their lawyer, Samuel Knight, would take their case to a meeting of the governor of the still independent state of Vermont and his council, which would be held in Norwich early that June.

They also agreed that Lucy, not Bijah, would plead their case. This lively woman, who was approaching sixty years old, had long captivated the neighborhood with her wit and shrewdness and with what her obituary later called "the fluency of her speech." So Lucy made the arduous journey on horseback, reaching Norwich, a town some 70 miles north of Guilford, on June 2, 1785, in time to see the grand procession of the governor and other dignitaries, escorted by the Norwich Cavalry in their scarlet uniforms.

A backlog of business meant that several days passed before Lucy's petition could be heard. Then, on Tuesday, June 7, she found herself in a village parlor, where the members of the council were seated in a semicircle, with Governor Thomas Chittenden presiding from a big desk in the center. No record survives recounting exactly what Lucy Prince told this august assembly on that June day. All we know with reasonable certainty is that the state's leaders listened to Lucy's eloquent petition for redress of grievances, and after acknowledging that she and her husband were being "greatly oppressed & injured" by the Noyes family, recommended that the town of Guilford take measures "to protect the said Abijah, Lucy & family in the enjoyment of their possession." The council further noted that if the selectmen of Guilford did not move quickly in this matter, the Prince family "must soon unavoidably fall upon the charity of the Town."

Lucy Terry Prince was born in Africa around 1730, where, at the age of five or so, she was captured and brought to the American colonies. Although we don't know her precise route, it seems likely that the slave ship that carried her across the Atlantic passed through Barbados before reaching Boston. There Lucy was purchased first by Samuel Terry—hence her last name. He later sold her to Ebenezer Wells, who took her to his home in Deerfield in western Massachusetts, where she served for more than a decade as his "servant," or slave.

Lucy was about ten and already fluent in English when she joined the Wellses, a childless couple, whose household consisted of Ebenezer, his wife Abigail, and another slave named Caesar. Besides her ordinary household duties, such as cooking and tending the kitchen garden, Lucy also worked in the tavern, which, for a time, occupied the Wellses' parlor.

Although, like other Deerfield slaves of that time, Lucy was considered a member of the Wells family, she was hardly treated as a social equal. At mealtimes, she and Caesar sat at a separate table, and on Sundays they were assigned to pews reserved for blacks in the meeting-house. It is said that when visiting Deerfield in her old age and invited to join her hosts at the dinner table, Lucy would invariably decline, saying, "No, Missy, no, I know my place."

Deerfield had suffered a long series of Indian attacks, including the great massacre of 1704, when the town was all but destroyed by the French. Lucy was about sixteen in 1746 when Deerfield endured the last of these attacks. The "Bars Fight" it was called, because it took place in meadows, or "bars," to use a colonial word, two miles south of town.

The only account of the "Bars Fight" that survives today is a poem of the same name attributed to Lucy. Whether or not she ever put its stirring lines to paper, the poem was apparently recited often enough in the town of Deerfield to be carried down orally through the generations. The earliest written version is found in an 1819 manuscript history of Deerfield, by Pliny Arms, a local lawyer. Not until 1855 did it first appear in print as a twenty-eight line poem.

Something of its vividness is conveyed in the following excerpt:

Eunice Allen saw the Indians coming
And hoped to save herself by running
And had not her petticoats stopped her
The awful creatures had not cotched her
And tommyhawked her on the head
And left her on the ground for dead.

Although no other verses composed by Lucy Terry Prince survive, these lines have an oral ring to them, making it likely that this young woman had inherited both the linguistic and poetical skills of her African ancestors, and produced other verses as well. Some have credited her with being the first American black woman poet.

While Lucy took for granted her lowly position in the Wells household, life was not all drudgery for this bright-eyed girl, who enjoyed a wide reputation in Deerfield as a vivid storyteller. Even soldiers passing through town and stopping for refreshment at the Wellses' tavern were entranced by the charismatic slave girl who brought them food and drink and often joined in their good-humored banter.

One such soldier might have been Bijah Prince, who—during yet another outbreak of war with the French in 1747—had joined a militia company in Deerfield, and thus on occasion likely frequented the Wellses' tavern. Wherever Bijah first met Lucy, it didn't take him long to succumb to her charms.

Born in 1706, Bijah Prince was a Connecticut native who had spent more than twenty years in Northfield, Massachusetts, as the slave of Benjamin Doolittle. Then in 1747 he was bought by a young man named Aaron Burt, who promised to free him. Within a few years, Bijah not only possessed his freedom, he'd also become Northfield's first black landowner.

During the ensuing years, Lucy and Bijah saw one another quite frequently. To be near her, whenever possible he took jobs that were in or close to Deerfield. It wasn't long before Lucy returned the affections of this man in his forties, described as having a "soft voice" and carrying "a big smile." When Bijah achieved the prized status of a free black property owner, there was little question that he was a decided catch for Lucy Terry. She could now dream of settling down in a house of her own and raising a family. All she needed to become Bijah's wife was permission from her owners, Ebenezer and Abigail Wells. By the spring of 1756 she had obtained it, and on May 17, the two were married, with Elijah Williams, a justice of the peace, performing the ceremony.

Shortly after their marriage, Lucy moved with her new husband into a small house owned by Wells just east of Deerfield village. Situated near a stream, still known today as "Bijah's Brook," tradition tells us that the newlyweds' home quickly became a gathering place for local youth who admired Lucy Prince's "wit and shrewdness" and came to "hear her talk," and presumably recite poetry as well.

By this time the French and Indian War was in full swing, placing Deerfield in danger once more of enemy attack. So, only a month after the Princes' wedding, fifty-year-old Bijah joined the Deerfield militia, under the leadership of Elijah Williams. There, for the next several months, he served as his unit's drummer. By the following January, no longer in uniform, he was home for the birth of his and Lucy's first child, a boy named Caesar. Sometime in the intervening months, Lucy had obtained her freedom, probably paid for with Bijah's salary. Thus the Princes now became one of Deerfield's few free black families.

Over the course of the next thirteen years, four sons and two daughters were born to the Princes. Hardworking and ambitious,

Bijah and Lucy would bring up their children to be proud, literate New England citizens. They also dreamt of living on their own farm. Not until the early 1770s, however, did this dream become a reality.

A decade earlier, Elijah Williams, Bijah's militia commander, had found himself caught up in the frenzy of land speculation sweeping over the region. At the end of the French and Indian War in 1763, the governors of both New Hampshire and New York began selling rights to land in the New Hampshire Grants, as today's state of Vermont was then called. A founder of the town of Guilford, a frontier outpost in the southeast corner of the Grants, Williams owned title to several hundred acres of the land handed out by Governor Wentworth of New Hampshire. There was a catch, however. By law, five acres of every fifty-acre lot had to be cleared, or Williams would lose the rights to his property. So, in return for a hundred of those acres, Bijah Prince frequently made the day's trip north on horseback to cut down the trees on Williams's land. Not until he had clear title to his own acres did Bijah begin preparing his fields for planting and erecting a house. It was 1775 before Lucy and the Prince children moved permanently into their new home.

Unfortunately, as the Princes soon found out, Guilford, despite its bucolic setting, was not a peaceful place. By 1777, land disputes—common for some time—between those loyal to New York State and supporters of the newly independent state of Vermont, had erupted into violence. While Lucy and Bijah were building and settling into their new home, their neighbor, John Noyes, was erecting a large pretentious house directly across the road. Greedy and intolerant as well as unscrupulous, Noyes, probably angered by the close proximity of the Princes and determined to acquire their superior farmland, began his persistent harassment soon after their arrival in Guilford.

By this time fighting between the colonists and the British had already broken out. In 1779, Lucy and Bijah's two eldest sons—Caesar, twenty-two, and Festus, fifteen—both enlisted, the latter joining his Vermont regiment as a fiddler. Barely ten days after the two had left home, their younger brothers, Tatnai and Abijah, were attacked and brutally beaten by Joseph Stanton, a close friend of John Noyes. The war between Noyes and the Princes had begun in earnest.

By the mid-1780s, Lucy and Bijah were suffering not only from persecution by their neighbors but also from the hard times following the Revolution. While harassment by Noyes abated somewhat after Lucy's appearance before the governor and council in 1785, two years later Bijah was forced to sell his Guilford farm to a friend and neighbor, Augustus Belden. Fortunately, Belden let the Princes stay on the land, and there Bijah died in 1794.

A story survives claiming that, sometime after her husband's death, Lucy tried unsuccessfully to get one of her sons admitted to Williams College, in western Massachusetts. While the college archives contain no record of such an application, by the time that institution opened in 1793, Lucy's two youngest sons, born in the 1760s, were well beyond the age of most undergraduates. Still, the apocryphal tale of her eloquent appeal before the college trustees is yet another testimony to Lucy's remarkable determination as well as her reputation as a public speaker.

In the last years of the eighteenth century, the Prince family was caught up in yet another land dispute, this time over property rights—obtained back in 1761 by Bijah—in Sunderland, a village northwest of Guilford. Following Bijah's death, Lucy and her children, having relinquished their Guilford farm to Augustus Belden, decided to resettle on Bijah's Sunderland acres. Upon arriving there, however, they discovered the property already occupied by Eli Brownson, who had been there for more than thirty years.

Apparently, Bijah's land, along with that of many of the other original Sunderland proprietors, had been illegally appropriated by speculators, and sold off at a handsome profit.

Late in 1797, Caesar and Festus, claiming the land as rightfully theirs, faced Eli Brownson in the Bennington county court. They lost this first round, but, exhibiting their now legendary family persistence, the brothers appealed the decision to the state supreme court, where two years later they won their case.

But matters did not end there. Soon Brownson himself was back in county court making charges against the Princes that are nowhere made clear. The case dragged on for another seven years, ending up in the state supreme court by 1803, with Lucy, now in her seventies, defending her family's rights with her usual eloquence and skill. In the end the judges made what they considered a fair settlement. They allowed Brownson to keep the land, but gave the Princes $200, a very large sum for those days.

Lucy, however, was not satisfied. Because she was the widow of one of the original proprietors, the town of Sunderland owed her a place to live, and she demanded that the selectmen come up with a satisfactory solution. Anxious to do well by this now legendary local woman, in 1806 the town purchased eighteen acres from Eli Brownson "for the use and benefit of Lucy Prince & her heirs." Lucy's sons settled on that piece of land, originally part of Bijah's lot, and Lucy was given another lot on which she spent her last years together with her ailing daughter Duruxa. As a recent biographer has noted, "She was poor but she was secure and at last the achievements of her husband were recognized by law."

Lucy lived for more than a decade after moving into the small house provided by the town. It is said that in these years she made an annual pilgrimage on horseback to Guilford to visit Bijah's grave and see old friends. Blindness overtook her in her last years, and she died in Sunderland on July 11, 1821, at the age of at least ninety-one. A long obituary published in the *Vermont Gazette* of Bennington disclosed that the funeral sermon had been preached by the Reverend Lemuel Haynes, then a noted Congregational minister, who, in 1804, received an honorary degree from Middlebury College, becoming the first black in the nation to be so recognized. No record survives of Haynes's eulogy for Lucy Prince, but he surely praised the extraordinary courage, dignity, and eloquence that had marked this gifted woman's long and remarkable life.

ANN STORY

1741–1817

Pioneer and Patriot

THIRTEEN-YEAR-OLD SOLOMON STORY STOOD LOOKING DOWN at the body of his father Amos, lying crushed under the huge maple tree he'd been felling with his ax. It was the spring of 1775, and the two had been clearing land in the Salisbury wilderness to plant crops. They had spent the winter constructing a small log cabin and soon planned to head back down the trail to Rutland to pick up the rest of the family: Solomon's mother Ann, and his four younger brothers and sisters. Now, suddenly, the boy found himself all alone—the nearest neighbor was two miles away in the town of Middlebury. He must bury his father and then walk the twenty miles to Rutland and give his mother the terrible news.

A less stalwart woman, upon hearing word of her husband's sudden death in the wilderness, would have turned around and gone back home to Connecticut, but not Ann Story. Instead, determined to carry out what she and Amos had planned together, Ann and her five children moved into the cabin Amos and his son had built near the banks of Otter Creek. They started the work of

ANN STORY

planting crops and began their new life in the territory then known as the New Hampshire Grants.

Little is known of Ann Story's early years, and indeed most of the accounts of her life are drawn from memories only much later set down by others and have about them the stuff of oral tradition and even legend. There is even a dispute among historians as to the actual time of her birth. But 1741, the date carved on her tombstone, seems the most likely. Born Hannah Reynolds in Preston,

Connecticut, she was one of six living children raised by John Reynolds and his wife Hannah and was called Ann to distinguish her from her mother. The Reynolds were poor, so poor that John spent his life working for other farmers, and all his children, including his daughter Ann, grew up accepting hard work as a reality.

In 1755 Ann Reynolds married Amos Story, another poor hired hand, who like Ann's father "worked out" for Connecticut farmers in return for meager wages. As her mother had, Ann struggled to raise and feed a growing family. Meanwhile, in the southern New England colonies, a mounting population and the rising cost of land held out little hope that the Storys could ever obtain a farm of their own. So, after nearly twenty years of working for others and scrimping by, they decided to move north to the mostly empty, heavily forested land that is now the state of Vermont.

When Ann and her five children arrived in Salisbury on foot, accompanied by a packhorse carrying their few belongings, they settled into the cabin that Amos and Solomon had built and began sowing wheat and other staple crops. They also fished and shot game for food. At the time Ann was thirty-three, a strong, fearless woman of keen intelligence. She soon learned that she would need all these good qualities in the months ahead.

The spring of 1775 was not a particularly auspicious time to take up residence on the banks of Otter Creek in Salisbury. While the town existed on paper (it had been chartered in 1761), settlement had been very slow. The only other white settlers at the time of the Storys' arrival were Joshua Graves and his family, who lived in a cabin half a mile away. The unbroken wilderness surrounding these two farms was filled with dangers, both from wild animals and from potentially hostile Indians. Furthermore, new arrivals like the Storys and Graveses felt little assurance that their property rights were secure. A dispute between New Hampshire and New York over who had the right to sell land in the Grants had been under way for some time. Added to this were the dangers from the war that had already broken out between the American colonies and Great Britain. In early May 1775 Ethan Allen and his Green Mountain Boys had captured Fort Ticonderoga, some twenty miles east of Salisbury in New York State, and by that winter, most of those who had built cabins in the settlements along Otter Creek had retreated to relative safety in larger communities further south. Joshua Graves and his family joined the exodus, leaving Ann Story and her five children alone in the wilds of the new town.

Once fighting erupted between the British and the colonists, the location of the Story cabin proved both a hazard and an asset. A hazard, because it was now on the front lines of the Revolutionary War, where the Green Mountain Boys were defending New England citizens against attack by British forces from Canada. And an asset because this cabin on the banks of Otter Creek—a major thoroughfare in the days before any roads existed—also served as an outpost for the patriots, a place where intelligence about enemy movements could be passed on and where rest and refreshment could be obtained.

Ann Story was eager to help these northern patriots and defend her new homeland against the claims of both New York and the British. "Give me a place among you," she is said to have told the Green Mountain Boys, "and see if I am the first to desert my post." Tradition also tells us that Ann "feared neither Tory, Indian, nor wild beast."

"The Widow Story," as she was locally known, taught her children to be equally brave and patriotic. Her sons often served as sentinels. There was that day in the spring of 1776 when one of the boys slipped quietly into the house to tell his mother that he had seen a pillar of smoke rising from the deserted Graves cabin. A cautious exploration of the site soon revealed that Indian raiders, who were fighting in alliance with the British, had burned it down.

Certain that their own cabin would be next, Ann and the children quickly removed everything of value and piled it into their canoe. Then, after the family had clambered in, they paddled across Otter Creek into the flooded shrubbery on the far bank, where they watched in horror as flames soared above their own cabin.

Once she was certain the Indians had gone, Ann returned to examine the charred remains of the home her husband and son had built. Such a sight would induce most people to carry their families to safety, but it only made Ann Story more determined to stay on. "If the smoking ruins of our home disheartened us," she explained years later, "the hope arose that the Indians had made so little in this excursion they might not visit the region any more. So we began cutting and laying up small trees such as the children and I could handle, and it was not long before we had quite a comfortable cabin . . . on the spot where the former one had stood."

There was, however, one important feature of this new cabin not found in the old, and this was a secret trap door. According to family tradition, it opened to reveal a rock crevice in the granite ledge underlying the cabin floor, which in turn led into a dense thicket of prickly ash. A path leading to the river had been hacked through the thicket to serve as an escape route for the family.

Given the dangers they now faced, Ann Story determined that a good hiding place as well as a way to safety was needed to protect her young family. After searching both sides of the river, she found a high bank on the western shore where they could hollow out a cave.

Working from their canoe, Ann and her older children dug a tunnel into the bank and slowly constructed a hideout. When finished, there was space for the canoe, and above the waterline they had built a wide shelf where they could store supplies and the family could sleep at night, secure from marauding Tories and Indians. Each morning they returned to their cabin on the opposite shore.

This secret cave had the added advantage of increasing the Story family's value to the Green Mountain Boys, who now had a place in this corner of the Champlain Valley to store ammunition and other supplies. Ethan Allen's men, impressed by this ingenious, resolute, and fearless woman, whose loyalty to the patriot cause was unquestioned, often dropped by the Story cabin to obtain both intelligence and advice from Ann. It was not long, tradition tells us, before she was able to prove her true worth as a spy.

One morning one of the Story boys came running to Ann with the news that he had found a woman alone and crying in the woods. After leading his mother to the spot, the two placed themselves where they could not be seen. Observing the woman carefully, Ann realized she was pregnant, and after making certain there were no enemies about, she and Solomon went up to her and persuaded her to return with them to their cabin. There the woman told of being captured by Indian raiders, who had intended to carry her north to Canada. She had been unable to keep up their pace, however, and was soon left behind to die.

The erstwhile captive remained with the Storys until after her baby was born, sleeping with them in their cave at night where the newborn's cries might be less easily heard than in the cabin. But muffling the sound proved difficult, and early one morning it was heard by a passing Tory named Ezekiel Jenny. Jenny, who probably knew of Ann Story's hiding place but not where it was located, decided to wait. As the day brightened, he saw her canoe slip out from its camouflage of bushes and cross the creek to where the Story cabin stood. When Ann stepped onto the shore, Jenny confronted her with his loaded gun and began pelting her with questions about the activities and whereabouts of the Green Mountain Boys. But Ann refused to be intimidated. "To all his threats I bid defiance," she later remembered, "and told him I had no fears of being shot by so consummate a coward as he." Eventually Jenny, realizing that he would get nothing out of the "Amazon Widow," slunk off down the creek in the direction of Middlebury.

Once Jenny was out of sight, Ann tore a sheet out of the family Bible (the only paper she had), scribbled a quick note of warning to the Green Mountain Boys, and sent Solomon off with it. Thanks to this information, Jenny and his fellow Tories were soon captured in Monkton, a settlement north of Middlebury, and delivered to patriot headquarters across Lake Champlain at Fort Ticonderoga.

Since their cave was unreachable by boat when Otter Creek froze over, the Story family spent the remaining winters of the war in the comparative safety of Rutland, returning to their farm in Salisbury each spring to plant and harvest their crops. Meanwhile, Ann's two oldest sons, Solomon and Ephraim, joined the Green Mountain Boys.

With the coming of peace in 1783, the family returned permanently to Salisbury where they continued to farm the land to which they now held a secure title. By this time, new settlers, attracted by the availability of cheap land free of wartime marauders, began pouring into Vermont. Even Salisbury's heavy forests were slowly cut down, so that by the end of the century, numerous small farms dotted the countryside.

One by one Ann's children grew up and left the farm. In 1792, a year after Vermont joined the Union, Ann married Benjamin Smalley, another early settler who had helped Solomon bury her first husband, Amos. Ann and Benjamin had thirteen years together before he died in 1808, leaving his widow in debt. But this determinedly independent woman, who would accept help from no one, supported herself by serving as a midwife and nurse to the sick and elderly.

Then in 1812, when the United States was once again at war with Great Britain, Ann remarried. This third husband, Stephen Goodrich, owned a prosperous farm in Middlebury, where she peacefully passed her last years, dying on April 5, 1817, at the age of seventy-five.

In the nearly two centuries since her death, Ann Story has inspired powerful memories. One old Vermont settler later described her as a "busting great woman who could cut off a two-foot log as quick as any man in the settlement." But the full story of this remarkable woman's life, gleaned from accounts passed down through the generations, depicts a pioneer who is remembered less for her brawn than her bravery and quick wit. Ann Story is a heroine because she used these qualities to forward Vermont's and America's struggle for independence.

EMMA WILLARD

1787–1870

Educating Women for the Republic

IT WAS HIGH SUMMER WHEN TWENTY-YEAR-OLD Emma Hart first glimpsed the town of Middlebury. The year was 1807, and she had been invited by the trustees of the local academy for young ladies to take charge of their school. This bustling manufacturing community in the Champlain Valley had recently been crowned by a small college, and was one of the fastest growing towns in the state. Though many log cabins still lined the village streets, Middlebury society, according to this young schoolteacher from Connecticut, was a dazzling affair. "I find myself in a very high state of cultivation," Emma wrote her parents soon after her arrival, "much more than any other place I was ever in. The beaux here are, the greater part of them, men of collegiate education . . . Among the older ladies, there are some whose manners and conversation would dignify duchesses."

Miss Hart's School had thirty-seven pupils when the term opened on August 20 in the academy building on Seymour Street. But Emma soon discovered that her job as preceptress was not going to be easy. For one thing, her days were oppressively long.

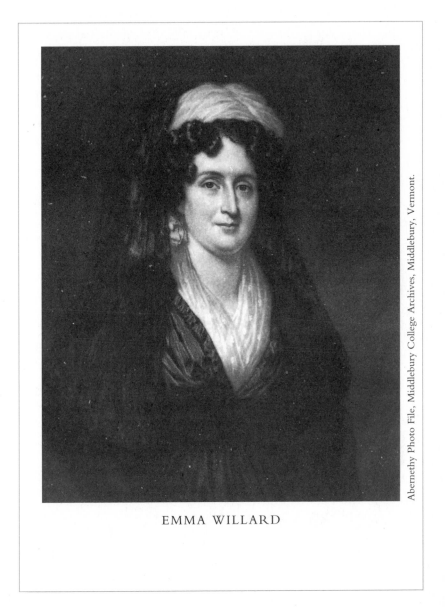

EMMA WILLARD

School began at nine with a break for dinner at one, then resumed until late afternoon. After classes had ended, Emma barely had time to go home and change before she was due out again, either for a religious meeting at the home of one of her pupils, or at a weekday service held by one of the four Protestant churches in town. Though she felt she had to attend these, she was frustrated at finding herself at the center of sectarian rivalries among her students' families; she confessed to her parents that "to please all is impossible."

Emma endured other difficulties that first year as preceptress, including the hardship of a particularly frigid Vermont winter. As she recalled many years later, "the weather was very cold, with frequent storms and much snow." Classes were held in a large oblong schoolroom whose only source of heat was a small fireplace on the north wall. When the cold was too much to bear, Emma would call her pupils onto the floor, and arrange them by twos for a country dance. Then the girls who could sing "would strike up some stirring tune," and Emma, taking one of the students as her partner, would lead the dance "and soon have them all in rapid motion." Only when everyone was warm did school exercises resume.

Despite the difficulties she experienced during her first year of teaching in Middlebury, her school proved a decided success. By the spring of 1808, enrollment had almost doubled in size and included pupils from different parts of the state. Emma Hart's career as an educator was well launched.

This native of Berlin, Connecticut, was born on February 23, 1787. She was the sixteenth of seventeen children who made up the family of Samuel Hart and his second wife, Lydia. "If the baby had been a boy," her father told the minister who was to christen her, "we would have named him for General Washington, but under the circumstances she will be baptized as Emma."

Whether Samuel Hart had made similar pronouncements at the christening of each of his daughters or not, he would develop a very special relationship with this one. Emma was a remarkably precocious child. An avid reader with a great hunger for knowledge, by the age of twelve she had taught herself geometry, a subject girls of the time were deemed incapable of mastering. Samuel Hart apparently encouraged all these scholarly efforts, telling Emma to ignore those who wished to confine women to a life of intellectual inferiority. He enjoyed discussing philosophy with her, and as she grew older he would often call her from her domestic pursuits to share a passage from a book he was reading or an essay he had written.

In 1802 Emma enrolled at the Berlin Academy. Two years later, at the age of fifteen, she was conducting classes for older children in her father's house. Then in 1806 she was given charge of the winter term at the Academy. Within the year Emma Hart's excellent reputation as a teacher had spread abroad, and in the spring of 1807 she received three offers to teach. One came from Middlebury, another from Hudson, New York, and the third, which she took, came from Westfield Academy in Massachusetts. She probably chose Westfield because of the school's excellent reputation. Hired as an assistant teacher, Emma soon decided that this subordinate position "cramped her abilities," and she left there after a term. With the offer from Middlebury still open, she decided to move to Vermont.

During her first term as preceptress in Middlebury, Emma had attracted the admiration of one of the town's leading citizens, Dr. John Willard. A physician and director of the Vermont State Bank, Willard was a religious liberal and a staunch supporter of women's education. When Emma had struggled that first summer with denominational rivalries that threatened the very existence of her school, Willard had come to her defense, relishing this young woman's skill and determination in outwitting her critics. Emma, in turn, was equally drawn to this older man who so willingly stood up for her, and the two were married on August 10, 1809. At the time John Willard was a prosperous man of fifty, who had four children from two previous marriages. But he proved a loving and supportive husband for Emma. Their only child, a son, John Hart Willard, was born September 10, 1810.

Once the Willards were married, Emma had no need to earn a living, so she resigned her position as preceptress and settled comfortably into a domestic routine in the large brick house her husband had recently built, which still stands across Main Street from the Middlebury College campus. While Emma herself was quite content with her new life, the proximity of this small men's college made her "bitterly feel the disparity between the two sexes," arousing in her an awareness of the advantages young men possessed in their pursuit of higher studies. This sense of women's intellectual deprivation was further heightened when her husband's nephew boarded with them while attending Middlebury College. Emma listened eagerly as he described his courses. She read his textbooks and even succeeded in passing an exam he gave her.

Emma and John Willard had been married for only five years when in 1814 financial disaster struck. It began with a robbery of the Vermont State Bank by someone using a false key. Suspected by the public of implication in the robbery, John Willard and the other bank directors were held personally liable and had to repay the $28,000 loss. Although the discovery years later of the false key in the bank's attic ultimately vindicated the directors, in the immediate aftermath of the robbery John Willard was forced to put heavy mortgages on his land.

This severe financial reversal had one positive outcome, however. It gave Emma a socially respectable reason for opening her own boarding school for girls in their roomy brick house. As she later recalled, "my leading motive was to relieve my husband from financial difficulties. I had also the further motive of keeping a better school than those about me."

If the Willards suffered a loss of social prestige resulting from John's suspected role in the bank robbery, enrollment in Emma's school gave little indication of it. When it opened in May 1814, her "Boarding School for Young Ladies," as it was initially called, included seventy pupils, forty of whom were boarders. The curriculum included English grammar, geography, drawing, painting, and embroidery.

Only gradually did Emma introduce the advanced subjects she deemed essential to women's higher education. When no dire effects followed from teaching her students mathematics, including geometry, she felt more forcefully the injustice of denying women the opportunity to obtain the best education available. Hoping to prove that young women were quite as capable of doing college-level work as young men, she asked that her students be allowed to audit courses at Middlebury College. This appeal, however, was denied by the college authorities. So was her request that she be allowed to attend examinations in order to familiarize herself with college teaching methods and standards. Such a presence, she was told would be "unbecoming" and might set a bad example.

In the end it was left to Emma herself to devise her own courses and teaching methods, and she dove energetically into the work. Long days of instruction were followed by nights spent studying new subjects, which, as she mastered them, were gradually introduced into the curriculum. At the same time Emma began developing what was essentially a teacher-training course. For the students who completed this, she found places and encouraged them to take charge of their own schools as soon as possible. It was in Middlebury, she later remembered, that "the stream of lady mathematicians took its rise."

Anxious to show that hard study would not undermine the health of her pupils, Emma included dancing and plenty of rest as part of their schedule. In the evenings she read aloud, and encouraged lively discussions on a variety of topics. This stimulating regime stood in sharp contrast to the rigid teaching methods of the day and helped to ensure the popularity of her school.

Conscious of her own success, Emma continued to wonder why nothing was "ever done by the public to promote [the education] of females?" Of course, part of the answer to that question lay in the contempt and hostility that the very idea of learned women aroused in some members of the opposite sex, including the authorities at Middlebury College. They feared, Emma realized, "that if women's minds were cultivated, they would forget their own sphere, and intrude themselves into that of men." The solution, therefore, was to find a way of developing women's minds that did not arouse male opposition, and to justify such an education not simply by proving that it was possible but also by showing—as a number of other women were doing at the time—that it was necessary for the future good of the new American nation.

Sometime after successfully establishing her own school, Emma began to put these thoughts together in a pamphlet entitled *A Plan for Improving Female Education*. Published in 1819, it took her nearly three years to compose her arguments for this piece, which declared that the future of the nation's prosperity depended on educating women. This argument had been around for some years, but her suggestion that public money should be spent to support higher education for women was a completely new concept. Dismissing the current mode of educating girls, Emma Willard's *Plan* underscored the importance of bringing them "to the perfection of their moral, intellectual, and physical nature."

It took Emma some time to come up with a suitable name for her ideal school. She couldn't call it a college, since giving an educational institution for young women such a name would have been dismissed at that time as an absurdity. Then one Sunday she attended Middlebury's Congregational Church and heard the pastor, Thomas Merrill, say a prayer "for our seminaries of learning." No sooner were the words out of his mouth than Emma realized she had the name for her school. "Female Seminary" not only sounded properly dignified, it was also unlikely to arouse male hostility.

By the time the *Plan* was published in 1819, Emma and her family were living in Waterford, New York, and she sent a copy to New York governor DeWitt Clinton, hoping that his state might decide to support a program of publicly funded schools for girls. Earlier she had tried to get Governor Van Ness of Vermont to agree to open a female seminary in Burlington, but that plan had fallen through. Governor Clinton was enthusiastic enough about her proposal to invite her to come to Albany and explain her *Plan* to a group of legislators. Aware of the unconventionality of a woman speaking before a large group of men, Emma dressed carefully for the occasion. Her gracious bearing and intelligence impressed her listeners, but they gave her no money.

Meanwhile, Emma found herself wooed by a group of enthusiastic and progressive citizens from the manufacturing town of Troy, New York, whose generous offer of support enabled her to open her Troy Female Seminary there in September 1821. So extensive was Emma's reputation as a teacher, her ninety students hailed from all over the Northeast and from as far away as South Carolina and Georgia.

By 1831 the Troy Female Seminary had more than three hundred students, nearly half of whom were boarders and the rest day students. So popular was the school that it was quickly evident that it could succeed without state aid. Emma, meanwhile began writing successful textbooks, one on geography and another on American history. Both were widely hailed and sold well, ensuring their author's financial independence.

At Troy Female Seminary, Emma continued the practice she had begun in Middlebury of training teachers, and she had soon established a flourishing teacher placement agency. What began as an informal network of alumnae, by 1837 had become the Willard Association for the Mutual Improvement of Teachers, whose members were able to spread her educational methods to other parts of the country.

Emma expected that most of her students, even those who taught for a time, would eventually marry and leave their teaching days behind. But she also understood that domesticity was not for everyone. As she observed in her *Plan,* some "ambitious spirits" cannot be confined to the household; they need a theater in which to act. So might she have described her own aspirations. But she meant it as a justification for encouraging young teachers to become professionals in their fields and use their talents and energies to establish and administer academies all over the country and even beyond. In sum, she had come to see and treat teaching as a serious professional vocation for women.

Dr. John Willard was in his sixties when he and Emma moved to Troy, where he died in 1825. Until his last days, he gave Emma and her school his full support, making himself indispensable as business manager and school doctor. After turning the Seminary over to her son John's wife, Sarah Lucretia Hudson, Emma returned to Connecticut in 1838. There she made an unhappy marriage with Dr. Christopher Yates, who turned out to be a fortune-hunter and gambler. In less than a year Emma had left him, and by 1844 she was back in Troy, living in a small brick house on the Seminary grounds.

Known by the students and faculty as "Madame Willard," to distinguish her from her daughter-in-law who was head of the school, Emma was kept informed of every happening and was a commanding presence at all major school events. Later she moved into an apartment on the ground floor of the Seminary building, where she could be near her son and his family. In her last years she called the students her "granddaughters," and when attending school receptions, occupied a big armchair as the girls processed by her, two by two, curtsying as they passed. She died on April 15, 1870, loved and revered by the Seminary community and cele-brated both nationally and internationally. In 1895 the Troy Female Seminary changed its name to the Emma Willard School. To this day it remains a highly respected boarding academy for girls.

CLARINA HOWARD NICHOLS

1810-1885

A Womanly Reformer

THE DATE WAS OCTOBER 15, 1851. A thousand people, including delegates and newspaper reporters, filled Brimley Hall in Worcester, Massachusetts, for the opening of the Second National Woman's Rights Convention (the first nationwide gathering had been held a year earlier in the same place). Among the speakers listed on the program was Clarina Howard Nichols of Brattleboro, Vermont. A journalist, whose articles in the *Windham County Democrat* on women's legal disabilities had been reprinted in newspapers around the country, Nichols was known to many in the convention audience. But this would be her first public speech since giving a student oration at Timothy Cressy's Select School back in 1828. Seated on the platform before this huge crowd, Clarina was understandably nervous. She later remembered Wendell Phillips, the noted Boston antislavery reformer, leaning over and whispering to her, "You must speak now, Mrs. Nichols."

Clarina filled her hour-long talk with stories of women who had been treated unfairly by the law. One of the most heartrending told of a single woman Clarina had known back home in

CLARINA NICHOLS

Townshend, Vermont, who lived alone and supported herself through her own handiwork. Then, in middle age, she married a poor but "worthy" (as Clarina called him) man. He was too feeble to work, so his wife became the chief breadwinner. Time passed and the husband died. By law, two-thirds of his estate went to his children by a previous marriage and only one-third remained for his widow's use. Even the house she had lived in with her husband passed out of her hands, and she was allowed to occupy only a small portion of it.

But this was just the beginning of the widow's troubles. One day she was found paralyzed in her bed, unable even to bring a spoon to her mouth. When her well-to-do stepchildren failed to take responsibility for her care, her fate was placed in the hands of Townshend's overseer of the poor. Since there were not sufficient town funds to support her, in the custom of the day, the paralyzed woman was auctioned off like a slave to the lowest bidder willing to assume care of her. Although in fact, at that time a poor sick old man could have expected no different treatment, this particular case was exacerbated by the widow's loss of property.

The women listening to Clarina that day knew of similar cases in their own towns, and when the story was finished the audience erupted into what one witness described as a "great sensation." Many more such stories followed, from accounts of wives unjustly treated by their husbands, to mothers being robbed of their children by law, and each was followed by a similar roar of applause. When her talk was over, Clarina's reputation as a favorite of audiences was well launched. Her grave yet conversational style combined with her abundant use of anecdotes would make her one of the most effective and eloquent speakers of the nineteenth-century woman's movement. Another secret of her success as a lecturer, a secret few were aware of, was that she knew herself what such unjust treatment was like. Thus Clarina's stories were not just tales but grew out of lived experience.

Clarina Howard was born in Townshend, a small village near Brattleboro, on January 25, 1810. She grew up in West Townshend, where her family was a prosperous one for the time. Clarina's father, Chapin Howard, who owned and operated a tannery, was a public-spirited man who served three terms in the state legislature, and many years as a town selectman, in which office he often handled poor relief. Those seeking aid from the town met with him in his own house, and Clarina later remembered some of those conversations. "While I sat in a quiet corner, an indignant and silent listener to revelations from the quivering lips of the poor . . . I saw my father's moistened eye and heard his regretful replies to the oft-recurring tales of sorrow." As Chapin Howard explained to his daughter, he was only the agent for a town whose citizens, like most other small communities in Vermont, evinced little interest in supporting paupers. Among them were many widows, who in those days lacked any property rights. Later in life Clarina would mark these overheard conversations as her earliest awakening to the legal barriers American women faced.

As the eldest in a family of eight, Clarina early assumed a responsible role in the Howard household. "Be a little woman and rock the cradle, and let Mama wash," she remembers her mother telling her when she was not yet three. Birsha Howard soon discovered her eldest daughter was a quick learner. Although Clarina was well trained by her mother in all the household arts, she became especially adept at needlework, including dressmaking and fine embroidery. In later life, knitting would become a trademark of her womanly persona. Whether working her needles and yarn while riding on trains, or at her seat in public lecture halls, she was rarely seen without her workbasket.

Clarina also received a good education for a woman of her day. At age three, she began attending district school, where she found it hard to sit still for six hours. But she also remembered taking "to learning like a duck to water." Her formal schooling ended with a year of advanced study at Timothy Cressy's Select School in West Townshend.

Blessed with a cheerful disposition, Clarina later remembered herself as a generous and impulsive child, "reckless of everything but the possible injury of the feelings of others." She grew into a striking young woman, whose intelligent blue-gray eyes looked straight into those of the person with whom she was speaking.

Clarina was twenty years old when she married Justin Carpenter in April 1830. Outwardly, he seemed the ideal husband for a well-educated young woman of that time. Born into a distinguished Guilford family, Justin, at age thirty, had recently completed his law studies at Union College. Filled with ambition but uncertain as to the form that ambition should take, he and Clarina made a choice shared by many other restless young New Englanders; they decided to seek their fortunes in the West.

In those days, "the West" for Vermonters meant upper New York State. The completion of the Erie Canal in 1827 had opened up a vast new territory for settlement, and the Carpenters chose to live in Brockport, a new community just west of Rochester. The future looked promising as Justin and Clarina plunged into building a new life for themselves. Their ambitions focused on the cultural life of this burgeoning frontier town. Justin and a business partner helped launch an academy and a town lending library. Clarina was hired to teach at the academy and began publishing a literary magazine, soliciting contributions of poetry and prose from the citizens of Brockport. The couple also threw themselves into the temperance cause, a popular crusade that reflected a concern not only over alcohol abuse but also anxiety about other aspects of early nineteenth-century American life. In March 1831 Justin and Clarina's first child was born, a girl named Birsha, after Clarina's mother.

Then, everything began to fall apart. Justin, whose business ventures failed, tried reading law. Clarina, meanwhile, began to take in sewing to keep food on the table. Soon her husband became abusive, and their marriage started on its downward spiral. "I had not a drunken husband," Nichols later confided to a friend, but her union with Justin suffered the same fate: "defeated purposes, one-sided love, and no support."

Little is known of the next few years. For a time, beginning in 1832, the Carpenters lived in New York City, but their fortunes fared poorly there as well. Clarina once again became the family's chief breadwinner, using her skill with a needle by contracting with a hatmaker to provide decorative stitching on a piecework basis. In the ensuing years, she gave birth to two sons, Howard in 1834, and Aurelius, known as Relie, in 1836. With three children to feed and house, their mother was more pressed than ever to make ends meet. There were even times when Clarina was forced to leave her children with relatives so she could look for work. The worst moment came when Justin carried the children off in what Clarina described as "a malevolent desire to wound her."

By 1840 Clarina was back home in West Townshend, having left Justin for good. Three years later she was granted a divorce by the Vermont Legislature, apparently with the full support of Justin's family. While Clarina surely felt relieved to be free of this destructive union, she was also aware that in a period when only one in a thousand marriages ended in divorce, she was in danger of being forever stigmatized as an undutiful and unsubmissive wife. The result was that few people outside her family even knew of Clarina's first marriage.

The publishing career that Clarina had launched in Brockport resumed in earnest once she returned to Vermont. First she confined herself to sending poetry to the local newspapers. When this proved successful, she began submitting prose as well. The *Vermont Phoenix,* in nearby Brattleboro, was the first to publish her articles. But soon the *Phoenix*'s rival, the *Windham County Democrat,* took her on as well.

George Washington Nichols, the editor of the *Democrat,* was a widower with six grown daughters when he engaged Clarina to write for his newspaper. George's correspondence with her first blossomed into friendship and then gradually took a romantic turn, at least on his side. While George, a shy, intelligent man, admired Clarina's genteel style and needed a wife, she harbored doubts about taking a husband twenty-eight years older than herself. In the end, however, she consented to become his wife, and the two were married in the parlor of her parents' house on March 6, 1843. Following the wedding, Clarina moved into her new husband's home in Brattleboro. For the remainder of his life George would give Clarina all the support, respect, and love that had been so lacking in her first marriage. The Nichols' union produced one child; a son, named after his father, was born in 1844.

Not long after the Nichols' marriage, George's health deteriorated, leaving him a semi-invalid. This meant that Clarina took over many of his duties as editor of the *Democrat.* Over the course of the next several years, while her husband's name remained on the masthead of the paper, Clarina gradually transformed the *Democrat* into a reform journal supporting such causes as temperance, antislavery, and woman's rights. At the same time she was in no hurry to have her new role as editor made public. First, she wanted her abilities as a political journalist recognized, while at the same time securing her reputation as a "womanly" editor.

Clarina once wrote a friend that she was "a walking storehouse of facts on the subject of women's wrongs," especially those of her own first marriage when Justin had spent her entire dowry and earnings, leaving her with no control over her own money. As she pondered these wrongs, she gradually came to realize that women could never obtain real security for themselves and their children unless they obtained economic rights. Beginning in 1847 she used the editorial columns of the *Democrat* to air her concerns and suggestions for reform. One Vermont legislator, impressed by the justice and lucidity of Nichols's arguments, took her ideas to the General Assembly then convening in Montpelier. There a limited women's property rights bill succeeded in passing that same year.

As far as Clarina saw it, however, this new law was only a first step toward providing women with full economic rights. Left unaddressed were the issues of giving wives control of both their earnings and their personal property. Gradually Clarina Nichols came to realize that the only way to obtain true economic justice for women was to give them the political rights needed to translate such justice into law.

It was this realization which prompted her to join the woman's rights movement and led her to attend the convention in Worcester in 1851, where she made her successful debut as a public speaker. It also propelled her into seeking partial suffrage rights for women from the Vermont lawmakers. To this end, in the summer of 1852, Clarina Nichols drew up a petition asking the legislature to give women the right to vote in school meetings. By fall, when the General Assembly convened, she had obtained 200 signatures, mostly from people in Brattleboro and a few other Windham County towns.

At a time when other women's rights activists, like Susan B. Anthony, were seeking full voting rights for their sex, Nichols advocated this partial measure both as an entering wedge in the campaign to give women full suffrage and as a way to enhance their role in the field of education. By 1850 women comprised 70 percent of the teachers in Vermont, and Clarina was filling the pages of the *Democrat* with articles extolling their fitness to teach and at the same time stressing their need for a better education.

When the legislature convened in October 1852, Nichols's school suffrage petition was referred to the House educational committee. Unfortunately, its chairman, Joseph Barrett, was known as a bitter opponent of women's rights, who would surely give the proposed measure a damning report. Lawmakers more friendly to Nichols's cause thus advised her to come to Montpelier and speak to the petition in person.

Clarina later remembered asking her husband if she should accept the invitation, and getting his "Yankee reply: 'Can you, have you the nerve?'" When she assured him she did but worried that such public exposure would give him pain, he responded that "there should be no reproach for the performance of duty." Still, Clarina feared the ridicule that might result from her speech, the first ever made by a woman before the Vermont legislature. Barrett was even ready when she finished her talk to present her with a pair of pants.

In the end the trousers never changed hands. Clarina Nichols went to Montpelier and delivered her speech on women's legal wrongs and the need for granting them school suffrage. She assured her listeners that voting in school meetings would not compromise a woman's femininity. On the contrary, it would simply extend a mother's accepted sphere of influence in the field of childhood education.

Total silence followed Clarina's concluding words, then the chamber erupted in a roar of applause and stamping of feet. Even her most outspoken critic, Mr. Barrett, was forced to admit that "with all her efforts, Mrs. Nichols could not unsex herself, even her voice was full of womanly pathos." A group of Montpelier women who had heard her speech from the gallery, came up to Clarina afterwards exclaiming that they hadn't known what women's rights were but now they were for them, adding that they would use their social influence to obtain justice for their sex.

By contrast, the legislators may have been pleasantly surprised by the tenor of her speech but they were not yet ready to give even partial voting rights to women. Despite this disappointment, Clarina was nonetheless pleased by the reception given her talk. Word of her skill as a genteel, womanly speechmaker quickly spread and she was soon in demand as a lecturer for both women's rights and temperance.

Clarina was a strong advocate of prohibition in Vermont and had lectured there so effectively that in the fall of 1853 the Wisconsin Woman's Temperance Society commissioned her and Lydia Fowler, an early woman doctor, to tour Wisconsin on behalf of a proposed state prohibition law. The two women lectured for four weeks without taking a day off. Of the Wisconsin tour Nichols would write that she enjoyed "the delightful collision" of argument and found the whole experience stimulating.

By the time the Wisconsin tour was over, Clarina, thoroughly smitten by the western fever, was determined to move her family to the frontier. She was prompted too by her advocacy of the Free Soil movement—which encouraged opponents of slavery's expansion to settle in the western territories—and was well-known as one of the movement's journalists. Clarina further saw such a move as an opportunity for her two eldest sons to obtain land. So, in the spring of 1855, George, Howard, and Relie joined the New England Emigrant Aid Society along with Clarina and left Vermont to live in Kansas Territory. When asked why she wished to bury herself on the prairie when she had only just launched her women's rights campaign in Vermont, Clarina had replied that it was far easier to adopt good laws in the organization of a new state like the one proposed in Kansas than to repeal unjust laws in "conservative old Vermont, whose prejudices were so much stronger than its convictions."

Unfortunately, troubles dogged the Nichols family's move to Kansas. Within a few months of their arrival, George was fatally injured in a farm accident. By August he was dead. Then in December 1855 came the Sack of Lawrence, as pro- and anti-slavery forces battled for control of the would-be state of Kansas. This eruption of violence sent Clarina back East for a year, where she supported herself by lecturing on behalf of both free-state Kansas and women's rights.

By the spring of 1857, she was back in Kansas, where, in the wake of their successful efforts to get rid of slavery, lawmakers were in the process of creating a progressive constitution. Thanks largely to the persuasive efforts of Clarina Nichols, this document would include school suffrage for women.

Except for a year in Washington during the Civil War, working for the Quartermaster General's office, Clarina spent the remainder of her life in the West. Poor health overtook her in the late 1860s, and in January 1872 she left Kansas for the more hospitable climate of Potter Valley, California, where two of her sons, George and Relie, lived. Despite the great distance that now separated her from her native state, Clarina stayed abreast of the news from Vermont, and when women obtained school suffrage there in 1880 she expressed her relief that her home state's legislature had finally "taken passage on the western train of modern civilization."

JULIA CAROLINE RIPLEY DORR

1825-1913

A Vermont Poet Laureate

ON THE MORNING OF AUGUST 15, 1877, the showers of the night before had laid the dust on Bennington's unpaved streets. Beginning at 9:30 a.m., a great procession of dignitaries—including President Rutherford B. Hayes and his wife—wound its way from the railroad station to the huge tent erected on the grounds of Fort Stark. The occasion was Vermont's dual centennial celebration of its independence and of the Battle of Bennington. The crowds were enormous—more than forty thousand, by some estimates. According to the *Burlington Free Press,* never had the little state of Vermont seen so many people gathered in one place at one time.

The ceremonies began with an address of welcome by the Honorable Edward J. Phelps, president of the Vermont Centennial Commission, and one of the most able lawyers the state ever produced. This was succeeded by a speech and an interlude of band music and concluded with the ode "Vermont," written especially for the occasion by Julia Caroline Ripley Dorr, who had made a name for herself as a leading New England poet. This lengthy

From a photograph by the Misses Selby

JULIA DORR

poem—341 lines long—was read, not by its author but by Professor J. W. Churchill of Andover, Massachusetts, whose voice, in the days before loudspeakers, carried easily over the great gathering of people. According to the *Rutland Herald,* "the effect of the poem was remarkable, melting many to tears, and then calling forth loud bursts of enthusiasm such as are rarely witnessed during the reading of a poem on such an occasion."

When the ceremonies ended, one Vermont farmer was overheard remarking as he emerged from the tent, "I would not take a hundred dollars for what I have got today." As the *Herald* reported, "admiration of Mrs. Dorr's poem is expressed by everybody, in all places."

Although Julia Caroline Ripley Dorr would spend most of her long life in Vermont, she had been born in Charleston, South Carolina, in 1825. Sometime around 1815 her father, William Young Ripley, had left the family farm in Weybridge, near Middlebury, Vermont, to seek his fortune elsewhere. He ended up in Charleston, where he quickly found employment in the dry goods business. Within five years he was earning enough to support a wife, and in 1822 he married Zulma Caroline Thomas, a woman of frail constitution, whose French parents had fled the 1793 slave insurrection in Santo Domingo to make their home in Charleston. There, in a house fronting King Street, William and Zulma's only child, Julia Caroline Ripley, was born on February 13, 1825.

This happy domestic interlude was short-lived, however. By the following spring, Zulma Ripley's health had deteriorated so badly that her husband decided to take his family on a trip north in the hope that it would restore her health. In early July the Ripleys boarded a steamer bound for New York City. While the sea voyage seemed to raise the sick woman's spirits, the relief was temporary. On August 2, 1826, only a few days after reaching the Ripley homestead in Weybridge, Zulma Ripley died.

With Zulma's death, the South lost its hold on William Ripley. Determined to make a comfortable fortune and then retire to his beloved Vermont, he moved to New York City, where he established a thriving firm of commission merchants. For a time Julia stayed in Middlebury under the care of a widow, Mrs. Hastings Warren, who, Julia later claimed, "gave me just the mothering I needed." Within the year, the two were called to join Julia's father in New York.

William Ripley's skills as an entrepreneur were such that it took him less than four years to accumulate a tidy fortune for himself. By early 1830 he and Julia, having left New York for good, were settled on a farm he had purchased four miles south of Middlebury. There, a year later, he married Betsy Warren, who would bear him three boys and three girls.

His daughter's early education consisted principally of daily recitations to her father as well as some formal schooling. Except for arithmetic, none of her studies gave her any trouble, and her favorite occupation was to curl up in the corner of her father's library and read whatever she could lay her hands on: "fiction, romantic history, travel—understanding much and guessing the rest," she later wrote.

Julia's intellectual talents were first publicly recognized when she was a pupil of eight or so in a Middlebury primary school on Pleasant Street. Thomas Merrill, pastor of the Congregational Church, and known locally as the "Puritan Bishop of Middlebury," was visiting the school, presumably to check on its pupils' progress. On that day, Merrill, who did not give compliments easily, singled Julia out for particular praise after she listed for him without a blunder all the rulers of England, from Julius Caesar through the kings and queens who followed, ending with the contemporary William IV.

The rest of Julia's education consisted of a term here and a term there in a variety of schools. Julia never forgot "the strange, narrow, cramped life" the pupils led in a Plattsburg, New York, boarding school she attended for a term. At mealtimes there were no chairs and the pupils stood while eating. Once, after failing to recite her lessons properly, she was told how fortunate she was that her father "was possessed of wealth and social position, as it was evident that [she] had neither beauty nor intellect, and would need whatever aid [she] could get from other sources."

In sharp contrast to this educational experience was the time Julia spent at the Middlebury Female Seminary, whose roots can be traced to Emma Willard's school founded back in 1814. At the time Julia first attended classes there, Nancy Swift headed the school. She was a "most inspiring teacher," Julia later remembered, who taught her pupils reverence "for all things high and holy." At the end of the day, Miss Swift, dressed in golden brown or pale yellow, would stand on a platform near the door of the school room, and curtsy to each of her pupils as they filed slowly past. "Could any girl help behaving well?" Julia later wondered.

Shortly after Julia first enrolled in that school, she was told in a hushed voice that one of the older girls was a poet. "Had I been told the Angel Gabriel was one of my schoolmates, I could not have been more overawed." Surely the thought that a mere seminary student might have some claim to literary distinction of any sort put ideas in young Julia's head.

Meanwhile, in 1837, William Ripley, bored with life as a farmer and longing once more to be in the thick of things, took over the management of a glass factory on Lake Dunmore. When that failed in the late 1830s, he went into the mercantile business in Rutland, then a market town and small manufacturing community set in the wide Otter Valley thirty miles south of Middlebury. In 1840 the farm was sold and the Ripley family moved into a stately and comfortable house in Rutland, known as "The Center."

It did not take fifteen-year-old Julia long to realize that, compared to the cultured community of Middlebury, with its college and Female Seminary, the bustling, commercial town of Rutland offered little opportunity for advanced study. Julia and four neighbors—including one boy—were determined not to waste an entire winter without school. They persuaded their parents to let them attend an academy on the second floor of an old town hall in a small nearby village. The single large room was "plain as a flagstaff," Julia later recalled, with rough, whitewashed walls, dingy blackboards, and rows of faded red desks. The more than fifty students were a "motley lot," but to Julia, they all seemed to share her ambition and love of study. And, while the one instructor, just out of college, was, in her words, no "marvel of learning," he was nonetheless a stimulating and inspiring teacher. In this rustic setting, for Julia study was "joyful labor."

Many years later she wrote of the haphazard nature of a girl's education in her day: "We went to school whenever it was handy, whenever it was quite convenient." Fortunately, Julia's hunger for learning led her to take advantage of any and every possibility that presented itself. She later remembered Latin as being "the most important subject" she ever studied.

From the very beginning, Julia was always a great reader, but it wasn't until she turned twelve that she began writing poetry. At first she said nothing of this for fear someone would read what she had written. To avoid detection she hid her verses away in odd nooks and corners of her father's house. "I sang for the pure love of it," she later explained.

Apart from reading and writing poetry, nothing is known of how Julia spent her time after she finished her formal schooling. By 1840 William Ripley had taken up marble quarrying and was well on his way to turning Rutland into the marble capital of the state, if not the nation. During these years, while he was building up his business, Julia met her future husband, Seneca Dorr, a young lawyer who worked for her father. The two were married on February 22, 1847, shortly after Julia's twenty-second birthday.

Little is known about the Dorrs' early married life, except that they lived for a time in Ghent, New York, Seneca's hometown. There in a large, old house that Julia christened "Greenholt," four children were born to the couple, one of whom died in infancy. A neighbor, who visited Greenholt as a child, remembered playing with Julia's stepbrothers and stepsisters, who often spent their long summer vacations with the Dorrs.

Despite a house to run and children to care for, Julia nonetheless managed to find time for her writing. Fortunately, when inspiration came, the words flowed out easily and she wrote quickly. It was later reported that she harbored "so great a dread . . . of becoming that social abomination, a 'blue-stocking,'" that she resolved never to close the door of her writing room to her children. Still, with Seneca's encouragement, Julia not only managed to produce some poetry but even attempted to sell some of her verses.

It is unclear when Julia first saw her work in print. By one account, only a year after her wedding she sent several poems to *The Columbian Lady's and Gentleman's Magazine,* a monthly literary journal published in New York. Two of these, "The Old Clock" and "The Spirit's Teaching," were accepted for publication, appearing in the magazine in 1848.

At about this time Julia also sent some of her poems to Lydia Sigourney—the "Sweet Singer of Hartford," Connecticut—whose sentimental and pious verses were then very popular, asking her what might be the best way to get them published. While Sigourney's response was complimentary and encouraging about the poems themselves, she nonetheless counseled her correspondent not to let literary endeavors interfere in any way with her primary domestic duties. She did, however, suggest that if, without neglecting any of her responsibilities to her family, Julia Dorr could "secure one hour" to herself daily "free from interruption," she should use this time for her writing. She also helped Dorr to get a poem published in *Sartain's Union Magazine,* a respected New York journal of the day. Since Seneca Dorr not only gave enthusiastic support to his wife's literary ventures but, on occasion, even sent her poems off to publishers without her knowledge, Julia was able to shrug off Sigourney's warnings against neglecting her wifely duties.

It was in the late 1840s that Julia wrote her first story, and after entering it in a competition, won one of ten $100 prizes. Other winners included such noted writers as Edward Everett Hale and James Russell Lowell. Receipt of this prize brought recognition and encouraged Julia to write more fiction. In 1854 she came out with a novel called *Farmingdale.* According to family tradition Seneca Dorr sent the manuscript, without his wife's knowledge, to a New York publisher, D. Appleton, which brought out not only the manuscript but also some of Julia's poems.

For reasons that are nowhere made clear, *Farmingdale* appeared under the pseudonym Caroline Thomas. The story, set in the neighborhood south of Middlebury where Dorr and her father had earlier lived, celebrates a plucky orphan named Mary Lester, who after her mother's death is sent to live with an aunt who treats her like a hired girl and shows little interest in providing her with an education. But Mary, despite many setbacks, secures a good schooling and eventually finds independence as the principal of a local academy. *Farmingdale* was only the first of many novels that Julia Dorr wrote and published in her twenties and thirties. Several of these were best sellers and ran to numerous printings.

Sometime in these years, when Julia Dorr was beginning to be recognized as a promising young writer, her father—himself a closet novelist—paid a visit to his daughter and son-in-law in Ghent. Surprised or not by Julia's literary success, William Ripley showed his pride in her accomplishments by leaving a folded sheet on the breakfast table containing a check for one thousand dollars.

After a decade in Ghent, the Dorrs, who by this time had three living children, began to tire of this rural backwater. Like many other easterners of the day they dreamt of better opportunities in the Golden West. So, after selling their house and packing up all their belongings, they decided to spend a few months in Rutland with Julia's family before heading for the Pacific coast.

Their lengthy stay at The Center, the Ripley family's Rutland home, did much to dampen Julia's initial enthusiasm for heading west. No sooner were she and Seneca and their children settled into the big house, already filled with her six stepbrothers and stepsisters, all still living at home, than Julia was overcome by her deep love not only for her family but also for the region where she had spent so much of her childhood. The thought of the permanent exile and separation from all this became too much for her to bear. Instead, she and Seneca—who would have to make a fresh start no matter where they went—decided to stay in Rutland.

After buying a piece of land less than a mile up Otter Creek from The Center, the Dorrs built a large house. Called "The Maples," it had views of Killington Mountain and Pico Peak to the east. There, a fourth child, Harry, was born in October 1858. For the next few years Julia Dorr's writing suffered as her time was absorbed not only by her four children but by the house and the laying out and planting of its gardens and orchards. Julia and Seneca would remain at The Maples for the rest of their lives.

Once Julia Dorr was able to resume her writing, poetry not fiction remained her favorite form of expression. Although largely self-taught, she had easily mastered the complexities of form, rhythm, and cadence, and was respected by the literary lights of her day as a competent and pleasing craftsman who employed a variety of styles on a wide range of subjects. At mid-century William

Cullen Bryant, one of Dorr's favorite poets, read her poem "The Bridal Veil," in *Sartain's Magazine,* and wrote to tell her how struck he had been by the pathos and beauty of its imagery.

Another admirer was Ralph Waldo Emerson. One summer, he even came to The Maples, while visiting the Rutland grave of his grandfather, who had served in the Revolution. At first Julia was rather in awe of the "Sage of Concord," but as her children began climbing on his knee, her shyness vanished. When Emerson published a collection of his favorite poems, he included one of Dorr's called "Outgrown."

But among the New England notables of the day, it was Oliver Wendell Holmes, famed author of *The Autocrat of the Breakfast Table* and a great talker, who became a particular friend. His first letter told her that he began his observance of Sunday by reading her poem "Friar Anselmo," which he claimed served him instead of a sermon. He particularly admired "the dignity, the finish, the melody of the verse you have given your audience in place of the cheap entertainment they commonly have to put up with."

The high point of Julia's career as a poet came in the 1870s, after she published "The Dead Century." Though the title may sound a bit grim to us, in fact this ode to the hundred years just completed exudes the progressive spirit of the day. Commissioned for Rutland's centenary celebration in 1870, it was recognized at the time as one of the strongest and best poems to emerge from the ferment of the centennial era, a spate of hundred-year commemorations a century after the Revolution. The ode's twenty-four verses glory in the great advances the world had seen in the preceding century, from the political freedoms achieved by the American and French Revolutions to the social advances brought about by the freeing of the serfs and slaves.

In the concluding verses Julia urges the centuries in their tomb to give this latest arrival room:

Saint or sinner, he did brave deeds
Answering still to Humanity's needs!
Songs he hath sung shall live for aye;
Words he hath uttered that ne'er shall die;
Richer the world than when the earth
Sang for joy to hail his birth.

Seven years later, when Julia was asked to write the centennial poem celebrating the Battle of Bennington and Vermont's independence, it was on the strength of this earlier ode that she was selected.

The poem also brought recognition from one of the great literary lights of the day, Henry Wadsworth Longfellow. After reading "The Dead Century" in the *Rutland Globe,* the popular poet wrote Julia Dorr that "though I have not the pleasure of your personal acquaintance, I cannot refrain from thanking you for the delight it gave me."

Julia Dorr did most of her writing in a little room adjacent to the big parlor, and overlooking the flower garden, which she called "her refuge and her inspiration." But she was much too interested in what was going on around her to shut herself away for very long. At first her children and writing absorbed most of her time, but as they grew up she became more active in the cultural life of Rutland.

In 1879 a group of Congregational Church women decided to widen the intellectual horizons of their sex by forming a society called The Fortnightly. Devoted to what we today would call continuing education, classes were conducted in such subjects as history and languages. When, at the end of the first year, the founding president of The Fortnightly resigned, Julia Dorr was nominated to be her replacement. Duly elected by an enthusiastic membership, she remained the much-loved and admired head of this society for the next thirty years.

Julia was active as well in the building of the first Rutland Public Library and served as president of the Rutland Free Library Association. When disagreement among its supporters erupted over the location of the new building, Julia with her usual "firmness and tact, succeeded in healing the breach."

Meanwhile, the Dorrs' long and happy marriage came to an end in December 1884 with Seneca's sudden death. At the time Julia was a vigorous women of fifty-nine, at the height of her creative powers. The two had not done much traveling together, so three years after Seneca's death his widow went to Europe for the first time, taking the daughter of an old friend along as a companion. On the ship to England they traveled in style, dining at the captain's table. Gregarious as always, Julia made friends wherever she went. In England they visited all the places she had learned about as a lifelong student of English literature and history. Best of all was the visit to Haworth, in Yorkshire. "One needs to see Haworth to understand the Brontës," she wrote home after this unforgettable experience. Back in Vermont, she published a number of popular travel sketches of England, Scotland, and Bermuda that provide lively accounts of their history and customs.

But it is Julia's poetry, not her novels or her travel writings, which stood the test of time and made her famous in her own day, when she was unofficially designated Vermont's "poet laureate." In June 1910, Middlebury College recognized her accomplishments as a writer by awarding her the second honorary degree ever given to a woman by that institution.

Julia Caroline Ripley Dorr knew the end was near when she celebrated her eighty-eighth birthday in the winter of 1913. "My dress is wearing out," she wrote in those last days. Her death came on January 18. In the many obituaries that followed she was hailed as the last of the generation of New England poets that had included such luminaries as Longfellow, Lowell, Whittier, and Holmes. As one reporter noted, "she retained her powers of expression to the last, having a sonnet in the current number of *Scribner's Magazine.*"

ABBY MARIA HEMENWAY

1828–1890

The Woman Who Saved Vermont's History

ABBY HEMENWAY WOULD LATER COUNT that mid–September day in 1859 as one of the worst she had known. Her trunk was packed, and so was her carpet bag. In half an hour the train would leave the Ludlow station, and she would be on her way north to Middlebury to begin work gathering material in Addison County for the first number of her proposed local history magazine, *The Vermont Quarterly Gazetteer*. But before she left Jewell Cottage, her family's house on Andover Street, the postman brought her a letter. Abby hadn't much liked the look of the envelope, and when she opened it she understood why. The paper inside was signed by several Middlebury College professors, all members of the Middlebury Historical Society. Thanks to their efforts, several town histories in that county were already being written. But in their letter these, "unbelievers at the College," as Abby dubbed them, made it very clear that they regarded her whole plan as "an impracticality . . . not a suitable work for a woman. How could one woman," the professors demanded, "expect to do what forty men had been trying for sixteen years but could not?" She would break down,

ABBY HEMENWAY

they predicted, before she had toured half the towns in Addison County.

"Middlebury had shut her door," Abby Hemenway later wrote, recalling that stinging rebuff. Not one to be put off by such dismissals, however, she thereupon set out to visit all the towns in the county on her own.

It is as editor, first of the *Vermont Quarterly Gazetteer* and later of the *Vermont Historical Gazetteer,* a five-volume compendium of the state's local history, that Abby Hemenway is chiefly remembered. As far as historians know, no one else in the whole United States attempted to do what she did—to collect and publish single-handedly the history of every community in her state. Over the course of her years as editor, Abby, who never married, persuaded, threatened, and cajoled hundreds of men and women to write the histories of their towns, churches, businesses, and schools. Hundreds more contributed memoirs of the early days of white settlement, or they provided sketches of forebears who had braved the terrors of the wilderness to build the first log cabins, where later stood farms and towns. Abby Hemenway succeeded in compiling all this material despite the many obstacles placed in her path, from money and legal troubles to floods and conflagrations.

Abby was the third of nine children born to Abigail Dana Barton and Daniel Sheffield Hemenway on their farm in the hills above Ludlow, a town nestled in the mountains of southeastern Vermont. Her mother, in addition to raising a large family, had gained a considerable local reputation as a poet. Young Abby shared many of Abigail Dana's tastes and talents, but she was not much help around the house. While at the age of six, her younger sister Carrie could already knit a whole stocking by herself, family tradition credits Abby with no such accomplishment. When it was her turn to dry the dishes, likely as not she would wander, dishcloth in hand, out of the house and down to her own private retreat on the banks of Jewell Brook. There she was free to dream or read her favorite books: accounts of purposeful men whose deeds had changed the course of history.

While Abby Hemenway acquired much of her early learning at home, she also attended district school. At the age of fourteen she began teaching school herself, and by eighteen she had saved enough money from her meager earnings to enroll at Ludlow's Black River Academy. There she received a classical training, which she later put to good use both as a teacher and as a writer. In one way or another, the education she obtained at Black River, combined with the support and encouragement she received from her mother and other family members, led young Abby to imagine that a literary career was not only appealing but also within her reach.

Abby was eighteen when she entered Black River in 1847. Short of stature and a striking, if not a handsome woman, she would be remembered for her intense blue eyes, straight brown hair, long slender hands, and most particularly her beautiful speaking voice.

Even as a student at Black River, she gave no hint that she shared the domestic dreams of the other female students. If she had beaux, there is no mention of them. And while she was certainly no recluse, it is hard to imagine her standing around with a group of schoolgirls discussing their marriage prospects. In any case, Abby likely realized that her literary ambitions and lack of interest in domestic matters made her an unlikely candidate for matrimony.

She remained at Black River Academy until 1852. While she seems to have accepted teaching as her chosen profession until something better came along, a certain restlessness marked this period in her life, as she moved first from one Vermont school-room to the next, later repeating this pattern when, in September 1853, she and a cousin headed west to the newly settled state of Michigan.

Little is known of Abby's four years out west, except that they were not happy ones. She particularly disliked the get-rich-quick atmosphere that she found there. "The Muses sing not to me in this land of realities," she wrote back home in 1854.

Abby was twenty-nine when she rejoined her family in Ludlow in 1857. Soon after her return she began work on a collection of Vermont verse, *Poets and Poetry of Vermont*. Exactly where the inspiration for this project came from, Abby does not say. Yet, there seems little question that her years in Michigan had inspired a profound nostalgia for the culture and traditions of her native state.

Published in 1858, this volume included not only the leading Vermont poets but also many who were unknown. Abby wanted, as she phrased it, to give voice to "those who claim no poetic name," and she saw poetry as a traditional way of passing down the values and folkways of northern New England.

Poets and Poetry was successful enough from the start to encourage Abby to embark on another editorial venture, one that celebrated the history as well as the literature of her native state. That was the ambitious decision to gather and preserve the history of every Vermont village and town, a task that would last her the rest of her life.

The job was not an easy one. In almost every community she visited, she met men who agreed with the Middlebury College professors that history was not suitable work for a woman. But Abby Hemenway's powers of persuasion were formidable, and in all but three of the towns she visited she found people to write, or at least to collect, the local histories of their communities. In each town she also engaged "lady assistants" to obtain subscriptions to the *Vermont Quarterly Gazetteer*.

The last leaves were falling that autumn of 1859 when Abby knocked on the door of Rokeby, a yellow frame house in northern

Addison County that looked west across some of the richest farm-land in the state to the distant Adirondacks. Rokeby was the home of Rowland T. Robinson, an elderly Quaker and Ferrisburgh town leader, who was also a prominent antislavery reformer and friend of the renowned abolitionist William Lloyd Garrison. As she entered the house, Abby couldn't help but notice the quantity of books lining the sitting room shelves. She saw too that it was not going to be easy to persuade the testy old gentleman who greeted her of the worthiness of her project.

Indeed Rowland Robinson at first showed little enthusiasm for Miss Hemenway's proposed *Gazetteer*. But Abby soon sparked his interest by telling him that Starksboro, a one-time Quaker commu-nity like Ferrisburgh, was supporting her work. When he asked if she had engaged William Worth to write the history of Starksboro, she was able to tell him yes. She topped this by adding that she had also engaged Henry Miles to write the history of the Quakers, once numerous in that part of the county. After she had listed some of the others who had agreed to write for her, Robinson was forced to admit that Abby Hemenway had won him over to her project and he assured her that she could count on Ferrisburgh. By her own account, he then credited her with devising "a most cunning plan. It appeals to all the pride in human nature," he acknowledged, adding that "no man will be willing to see all the towns in the county rep-resented and his own left out . . . and when a county is finished, it will awaken a county pride and when a few counties, a state pride." He concluded by telling her how pleased he would be to see her succeed, assuring her that the Quakers believed in women's rights. When Abby disclaimed entertaining any such radical sympathies, he replied simply that "thee knows too much to admit it; but thee does what is better than to say it, thee acts it." By the end of their conver-sation, Rowland T. Robinson had made it clear that he knew what Abby Hemenway was about perhaps better than she did herself.

Not until the very end of her tour of Addison County did Abby screw up her courage and visit Middlebury to ask once more for help from the historical society there. As if to prove Rowland Robinson's astute prediction, Abby found its members so impressed with her remarkable success that they gave in with good grace and agreed to assist her.

The first issue of the *Vermont Quarterly Gazetteer,* the Addison County number, was duly published on July 4, 1860, "a patriotic work for a patriotic day," Abby later called it. Despite this promising start, the second number of the quarterly, covering most of the towns in Bennington County, wasn't published until more than a year later. Similar delays marked the remainder of the *Gazetteer's* publishing history. A principal reason for these delays is that, while Abby was very successful at gathering historical material, she was not a good fund-raiser. Finding enough money to pay her printers remained a chronic problem. Her plan was to raise money through subscriptions, but she consistently overestimated the number of Vermonters who might be willing to pay for her magazine.

The longest break in the publication of the *Vermont Quarterly Gazetteer* came during the Civil War, when Vermont's heavy financial commitment to the war effort, combined with rising inflation, meant that subscriptions failed to keep up with printing costs. By 1864 production of the *Gazetteer* had slowed considerably.

It was at this point, and perhaps in part to compensate for the great vacuum in her life, that Abby found herself drawn to leave the Baptist church of her childhood and become a Roman Catholic. This decision was partly induced by a deeply felt piety that already during her adolescence inspired her to begin writing a poetic life of the Virgin Mary. Another factor influencing her decision was the reading she did for the *Gazetteer* on early Vermont Catholic converts, including Fanny Allen, the daughter of Revolutionary War hero Ethan Allen.

When the Civil War ended in April 1865, Abby Hemenway was thirty-six, without a settled future and as yet no prospect of resuming the editorship of the *Gazetteer.* Later that spring she went west to Notre Dame, Indiana, hoping to find a job at St. Mary's, the small Catholic women's college there. Although she was asked to contribute to a newly published weekly, *Ave Maria,* no permanent position was offered her, and by late summer she was back home in Ludlow.

The following year, 1866, Abby suffered the loss of her much beloved mother. That fall, she moved north to Burlington, Vermont's largest city, and there her fortunes improved. One Sunday after church, she was introduced to Lydia Clarke Meech, an elderly widow and fellow Catholic convert. The younger woman needed a home and the elder woman needed a companion. Sometime in late December 1866, Abby moved into the Meech house on Pearl Street for the winter. "You were the best Christmas present I ever had," Lydia Meech later told her new boarder, and what began as a temporary arrangement was soon accepted as permanent. Abby lived with the widow until Meech's death in 1874. By the spring of 1867, Abby was secure enough in her new home to resume her editorship of the *Gazetteer.*

When work was halted in 1864, six numbers of the *Quarterly Gazetteer* had been issued and five additional numbers had been set into type. J. Munsell, Abby's printer in Albany, New York, had been sitting on them ever since. All Abby needed, apparently, was enough money to pay off her debts to the firm, and the remaining histories could be printed. Whether she obtained the necessary funds from loans or gifts, by the late summer of 1867 the five issues were finally in print.

In addition, early 1868 saw the publication of the first of the five bulky volumes of the *Vermont Historical Gazetteer.* Volume I contained all the issues of the *Quarterly* published thus far: the town histories of Addison, Bennington, Caledonia, Chittenden, and Essex Counties.

The appearance of this hefty book with its twelve hundred pages solidified Abby Hemenway's reputation as an editor. Until now, her publication had been sporadic enough to inspire little confidence that she would ever complete the work. Now, however, the issuance of this first fat volume convinced her readers that completion was indeed possible. The book was praised both inside and outside Vermont, and now town after town agreed to prepare its history.

Unfortunately, the period of happiness and relative prosperity that Abby enjoyed in these years ended in 1874 with the death of Lydia Meech. The loss was a devastating one, although for a time Abby was not without a home, for Mrs. Meech had left her a life interest in the Pearl Street house. Then early in 1875 the dead woman's will was contested by a stepson. For the next four and a half years, Abby devoted a good portion of her time and energies to the ensuing legal battles. In the end the case was settled out of court in her favor, but the costs still forced her to part with the house.

Meanwhile, financial problems continued to plague publication of the *Gazetteer*. By the late 1870s, Abby was so deeply in debt to her printer that she was forced to ask for state aid to continue publication. While she did receive a few hundred dollars from the legislature, this was not enough to keep the work solvent. Then in the winter of 1882, shortly after the publication of Volume IV of the *Gazetteer,* Abby discovered that several hundred copies of the book had missing pages. When her printer insisted that she pay for the defective copies because she owed him money anyway, Abby refused. He then confiscated all the copies of Volume IV in her possession, claiming they were his property until she paid. But she responded a few nights later by sneaking into the building where the books were housed and "reclaiming" the confiscated volumes.

This action only led to more trouble. Abby was forced to mortgage the fourth volume to help cover her debts and never did regain ownership of it.

These miserable experiences drove Abby back to Ludlow. Her plan, since she could no longer afford a printer, was to rent rooms and set up her own publishing establishment. By January 1884 she managed to lease a large room on Main Street, which she divided into separate spaces, partitioned by "turkey red" curtains, for living and for printing.

In this makeshift setting Abby carried on her work, engaging relatives and friends to help her set type. Having no frame or stand in which to set her type cases, she sat on the floor "working day and night," a cousin remembered, "and scarcely eating in order to fulfill her contracts."

For six weeks or so during the cold snowy winter of 1884, Abby and her helpers made steady progress with Volume V. Then in late February Abby was run over and injured by a sleigh. Worn out with work, and suffering from pneumonia at the time of the accident, Abby nearly died. Recovery was slow, and in the spring on her doctor's orders she left Vermont for what was originally intended as a four-month vacation. She ended up in Chicago and decided to settle there, finding the atmosphere more congenial than being hounded by creditors in her home state. For the next five years Abby continued her work for the *Gazetteer* and supported herself by selling bound copies of individual town histories. In 1890 she died of a stroke. She was sixty-one and had continued working to the very end.

At the time of her death, four volumes of the *Vermont Historical Gazetteer* had been published. One more, including the histories of Windham County, appeared in 1892. But the manuscripts of Windsor histories (including her hometown of Ludlow), destined for Volume VI, were destroyed, along with all her papers, in a fire in North Carolina in 1911.

More than twenty years after Abby's death, the Vermont legislators, whose predecessors had been so reluctant to give the *Gazetteer*'s editor more than a few hundred dollars, voted to spend more than $12,000 simply to publish an index of her vast work. Perhaps the ultimate irony lies in the wording of the 1914 report of the Vermont Historical Society's librarian. Having described the *Gazetteer* as the greatest extant work on the founding of Vermont, he then complained of the enormous difficulty of compiling an index to the *Gazetteer,* noting that it "has all along seemed too prodigious for any man to undertake." Yet it was one woman, Abby Maria Hemenway, who defied the incredulity of the Middlebury College scholars and compiled not only the history of Addison but of every other county in the Green Mountain State.

RACHAEL ROBINSON ELMER

1878-1919

Independent Artist

ONE SUMMER DAY IN THE CLOSING YEARS of the nineteenth century, Rachael Robinson sat in the library of Rokeby, her family's house in Ferrisburgh, looking over a collection of small diaries, yellowed with age. These had been recently acquired by her novelist father, Rowland E. Robinson. Rachael, who was home from school for vacation, and curious about these relics of someone's past life, asked her father about them. They were, he told her, the journals of a Quaker woman, Marah Rogers. As a boy, Rowland had once traveled up into the hills east of Rokeby to the Rogers's weathered farmhouse and remembered Marah as a "plain reticent woman." When the diaries were found, years after Marah's death, Rowland had taken them for his library, likely viewing them as potential material for his highly acclaimed stories of early Vermont.

When Rachael began reading the earliest of these faded journals, she discovered that sixteen-year-old Marah was preparing to leave home to spend the summer term at the Nine Partners School, a Quaker coeducational boarding school in Poughkeepsie, New York—or, as Marah spelled it, "Pokipsy." Before Marah departed,

RACHAEL ELMER

she had learned to weave a blue-and-white checked apron and had made a suitably plain dress for the long stagecoach journey. By the time she returned from Nine Partners a few months later, Marah was a skilled seamstress, but her life's great adventure was over. The rest of her years were spent on her family's Vermont hill farm caring for her father and brother. After her death, all that remained of Marah's artistry was a piece of faded embroidery with the initials M.R. worked into its center.

The contrast between Marah Rogers's life, her "lonely womanhood," as Rachael later described it in a school essay, and the life Rachael herself would lead as an artist and illustrator in New York, could not have been more pronounced. Both Rachael's parents gave their daughter the freedom to be what she wanted to be. But perhaps this story of a Vermont woman trapped in a rural backwater had helped convince Rachael that, much as she loved Rokeby and Vermont, she was not going to suffer the same fate as Marah Rogers.

The first Robinsons to settle in Ferrisburgh—Thomas E. and his wife Jemima—had emigrated from Rhode Island in 1791, the year Vermont became the fourteenth state admitted to the Union. Members of the Society of Friends, they had chosen Ferrisburgh because a small Quaker community was already establishing itself there. Profiting from the sheep craze of the early nineteenth century, the Robinsons's six-hundred-acre farm prospered, allowing the family to enlarge their modest farmhouse by adding a plain wing in the Federal style. Named Rokeby, after Sir Walter Scott's popular poem, the house still stands on a hillside where it once boasted an unimpeded view over rich farmland to Lake Champlain and the Adirondack Mountains beyond.

It was Thomas and Jemima's son, Rowland T. Robinson, who inherited the farm and put Rokeby on the map as a refuge for fugitive slaves fleeing north to Canada and safety. Many years later,

Rachael, as a schoolgirl, wrote an essay in which she described the little chamber under the eaves at the back of the house where the escaping slaves lived. Until recently, traditional folklore considered this room one of the many secret hiding places on the Underground Railroad, but in truth there was nothing secret about what was called the "slave's room." As Rachael herself noted, the fugitives often spent several months in her grandfather's house working as laborers on the farm until passage to the safety of the Canadian border fifty miles to the north could be secured.

Rachael had no memories of her grandfather, since he died the year following her birth. But, beginning in the 1830s, Quakers had participated in the abolition movement in which Rowland T. Robinson had been a leader. While he resigned his membership in the Society of Friends because of the divisions that led to its refusal to openly support immediate emancipation of the nation's slaves, Rowland T. passed on to his family, including his granddaughter Rachael, a strong Quaker spirit that lauded hard work, frugality, and social responsibility.

Rachael's artistic gifts were an inheritance from both her parents. Her father, Rowland E., had begun his career as a painter and illustrator, but by the time Rachael was born in 1878 he was making a name for himself as a popular writer of rural sketches. Her mother, Anna Stevens Robinson, had wanted to be an artist herself until marriage and motherhood forced her to lay those dreams aside. Instead, she transferred her ambitions to her eldest daughter. When Rachael was only three, Anna began giving her art lessons. At the age of eight, Rachael received a gift of sketchbooks from her father.

It hadn't taken Rowland and Anna long to realize that their eldest daughter was an exceptional child. Her artistic talent, visible at an early age, was matched by a remarkably lively and pleasing personality. Though she was consistently held up as an example to her younger siblings, this incited surprisingly little if any resentment on their part. Rachael was simply too good-natured.

In 1890, when Rachael was twelve, she enrolled in a Chatauqua Art League Correspondence course. After she had studied two years, the program's director, Ernest Knaufft, recognizing that Rachael's talent surpassed that of most of his thousands of students, invited the fourteen-year-old to come to New York City and study in his life class. For the next three summers, with the full support of both her parents, Rachael spent a month or more attending Knaufft's drawing classes and growing increasingly attached to life in New York City.

At the same time, her parents did not neglect her formal education. When she was sixteen she left home to attend Goddard Seminary, a progressive, coeducational preparatory school east of the Green Mountains in Barre. To help pay her daughter's tuition, Anna, working out of their home, took on the position of Ferrisburgh town clerk. Soon after Rachael left for school, Anna reminded her in a letter that "Thee must not do as the rich girls do. . . . Thee is not at school for pleasure, but for improvement, though you may be sure we wish it to be as pleasant as possible."

During the three years Rachael spent at Goddard she worked hard developing her talents, from music and public speaking to writing and, of course, art. By the time she graduated she had learned to recite with great dramatic effect, winning the first prize in a speaking contest. Writing also came easily to Rachael and she became an editor of the school paper. Mathematics, however, proved a challenge. In letters home Rachael complained to her mother that she "despaired of mastering algebra." Eventually she grasped enough to pass the course, but only after considerable complaining about work and teachers.

Among her fellow students Rachael was a decided favorite. Years later they remembered her "demure manner, her quaint method of speech, her deep interest in everything connected with school life, and her eagerness to be of service." On warm evenings Rachael would often sit with her guitar on the front steps of the school and sing familiar old songs, while a surrounding group of students joined in the chorus.

Upon graduation from Goddard in 1894, Rachael considered making music her career, but in the end art won out. For a time she combined semesters of teaching in Vermont, including a drawing class at Goddard, with a month or so in the summer spent studying art in New York. But after two years, Rachael's parents thought she was spending too much time teaching and not enough studying. For three winters, beginning in 1898, Rachael, with Rowland and Anna's full support, lived in New York, where she enrolled in the Art Students' League.

The League had been founded back in 1875 by a group of young students from the National Academy of Design, then the only art school in Manhattan. The Academy clung to the formal, some would say rigid, conventional ways of teaching art. But many of the students there had witnessed the breakdown of the old academic system in Europe firsthand and wanted the freedom to innovate while at the same time to establish a serious art school. Life classes with live models were the most popular offerings of the League. Other available courses included portrait painting, composition, and sketching. Unlike other art schools, the League gave students the freedom to choose their courses.

That first winter of 1899, Rachael took a drawing class with Kenyon Cox, the new director of the League. She described this class in a letter home to her mother. First, the students placed their drawings on chairs in a circle to be judged, then "the great instructor" would stroll around and give numbers to the best ones. "[To] get no. 1 is a high honor," Rachael told her mother. She added that, while the men in the class tended to "fool around and sing and play jokes and give treats and loaf," the women plugged away "as mum as owls." Yet when the exhibition was held at the end of each term, it was the men, Rachael reported, "who come out with the good work."

What Rachael didn't tell her mother was that women art students often suffered discrimination from their instructors as well as their fellow students. Portrait classes, for example, were looked down upon as "women's classes." Nor was it unusual for a woman to be told she should be at home caring for her family rather than taking up classroom space.

Rachael's good nature may have spared her such treatment, but, like all League students, she learned to put up with her share of criticism from Kenyon Cox and the other League instructors. She learned too that such criticism was only a goad to work harder, which she did. After two years of study Rachael could report that Cox had not only given her "a beautiful criticism," including a "charming little talk on drawing and draughtsmanship," but he had also rated her drawing a no. 2. "He really is quite human," she assured her mother.

After three winters at the League, Rachael returned home to Vermont, where she taught art for two years at Goddard Seminary. By 1906 she was back in the city, this time not to study but to earn a living, a challenging prospect for any young artist, man or woman. In Rachael's case hard work and determination paid off. That first year she not only found employment designing book covers for a firm called Decorative Designers, but she contributed illustrations for magazines such as *Youth's Companion* as well as for book publishers such as Harper's. The income from such work was barely sufficient, however, even for Rachael's modest needs. She often had to share a rented room and was grateful for food packages from Rokeby containing such delicacies as the farm's own creamery butter and beef.

Rachael began her life as a working woman artist by living in Greenwich Village. While looking for employment, she continued to take classes at the League, writing home that she had befriended several fellow art students, including "a Miss Wright and a Miss Darwin who are pleasant and quite my kind." Alice Morgan Wright would become one of America's first cubist sculptors.

Indeed, Rachael had a large circle of friends in the city. One fellow artist later remembered how she "always left such a vivid impression of her personality upon even the chance acquaintance." Perhaps this explains the many free tickets Rachael was given to plays and concerts, even the opera. When she could spare time from her work she frequently visited Manhattan's many museums and galleries.

By February 1907, Rachael was receiving enough commissions from some of the bigger publishing houses, including Harper's, to enable her to quit her job at Decorative Designers. Three years later, her earnings from one volume of illustrations alone made it possible for her to go abroad. On April 6, 1910, she sailed from New York to Naples and for the next four months traveled first through Italy, then on to Paris and London. Rachael's letters home displayed a wide-ranging curiosity about everything she saw and heard, from sculpture and architecture to the language and customs of the people.

Within a year of her return from Europe, Rachael was engaged to be married. She very likely met her banker husband, Robert A. Elmer, while boarding with his mother in New York at 189 Lenox Avenue. At the time Robert was a widower with two grown children.

The two were married in a simple ceremony held at Rokeby on October 27, 1911. As she had written her brother when he got married back in 1907, "It doesn't suit people in our circumstances to make a great splurge at the beginning." After the wedding she and Rob returned to New York where at first they lived on their own in a small apartment. When Rob was unemployed for a few months in the spring of 1913, they moved in temporarily with his mother on Lenox Avenue. Meanwhile, Rachael kept busy with her work, while throwing herself with zeal into the business of housekeeping, which included taking cooking classes at the Young Women's Christian Association. As one contemporary said of her, "Mrs. Elmer is a living refutation of the popular illusion that artists are by temperament impractical."

By the end of the summer of 1913 Rob had presumably found work, since early September saw the couple living in their own apartment on West 122nd Street, a location that particularly pleased Rachael because of its proximity to Columbia University, the Hudson River, and Morningside Park. By this time she was earning enough to afford a studio of her own in the same apartment building. She also enjoyed the help of a college girl who came every weekday morning for $1.50 per day to wash the breakfast dishes, make the bed, and clean the front rooms.

Meanwhile, a friend sent Rachael a painted postcard from London called "The Thames at Twilight." The message urged that Rachael do something similar for New York. "Our city is surely as lovely, and thee could serve her well," the friend added. Postcards were enormously popular at that time, and the idea appealed to Rachael as a good way to make money. So she created a series of impressionistic watercolor paintings depicting such familiar New York landmarks as the Statue of Liberty, the Woolworth Building, and the Brooklyn Bridge. Selling the idea, however, wasn't easy. Rachael claimed she "wore out three pairs of shoes taking the designs around to publishers before the P.F. Vollard Company of Chicago finally accepted them." Published in 1914, the set of six postcards, called "Art Lover's New York," was an immediate success and soon became the standard for artistic cards at that time.

Two years later Rachael produced a second set of postcards, this time made from woodblock prints. This "Biennial New York" series was used by the General Federation of Women's Clubs as official cards for their convention held in New York in 1916. Further recognition for her work came when in 1915 the Association of Women Painters included her postcard designs in an exhibition at the Municipal Art Gallery in lower Manhattan. Meanwhile books illustrated by her continued to be published by Harper and Brothers, Little Brown & Company, and the American Book Company.

Rachael was at the height of her success as a commercial artist when the United States entered World War I in 1917. Her Quaker heritage of social responsibility came into its own, but its pacifism did not prevent her from producing life-size posters for the war effort, or from visiting hospitals, helping to serve soldiers in canteens, and planting a large "war garden" in a plot outside the city. She and Rob also entertained servicemen in their apartment. Finally, at the close of the war, she designed a card for the Bird and Tree Club, proceeds from the sale of which were used to plant trees in war-torn France.

A brief reprieve from all this wartime activity came in August 1918 when she and Rob left Manhattan for a visit to relatives in Waverly, New York, not far from the Pennsylvania border. Perhaps one reason why they left the city was to escape, at least for a time, the ravages of the great influenza epidemic that in 1918 had been taking lives by the thousands in big cities all across America. Back in New York that fall, Rachael wrote her sister Molly of the havoc the flu was wreaking in the city—"we hear of sickness on every side," she told her sister. At the same time rumors were rife about the causes of the epidemic. Rachael reported that she and Rob had been told not to take aspirin "as it has been found tampered with, and filled with influenza germs—nice little trick of the Germans."

What she did not know was that the likely carriers of the disease were the very soldiers she had been nursing in one of Manhattan's overcrowded hospitals or entertaining in her apartment.

All that is known is that a few months later Rachael very suddenly became seriously ill, that doctors and nurses worked assiduously to save her, but their efforts were to no avail. Within twenty-four hours Rachael was dead.

When Rachael Robinson Elmer died on March 12, 1919, she was only forty years old, a gifted woman artist at the height of her powers, whose life, like that of so many other flu victims, had been cruelly cut short. What she might have achieved, had she lived, will never be known. Today examples of her work can still be seen at Rokeby in Ferrisburgh. Now a museum, it keeps alive the memory of the Robinson family, whose home it once was.

DOROTHY CANFIELD FISHER

1879-1958

Novelist and Crusader

DOROTHY CANFIELD FISHER DATED HER INITIAL INSPIRATION to become a writer to the spring of 1900. A twenty-year-old graduate of Ohio State University, she had accompanied her artist mother, Flavia Canfield, to Madrid, and was standing in a long, cold, empty gallery in the Prado Museum studying the portrait of a court dwarf by the great Spanish painter Velasquez. Dorothy recalled gazing deeply into the "dark tragic eyes" that stared out at her from the adult face of this stunted man. There she read a "wordless message" that filled her with an acute awareness of the human condition and a longing to share that awareness with others.

One of her early stories, "The Bedquilt," tells of a Vermont spinster, Aunt Mehetebel, who, as Dorothy later described her, was as "helplessly starved as the Spanish dwarf of what all human beings need for growth." A plain woman without money or a husband, Aunt Mehetebel had spent her life being alternately ignored or mocked by those around her. Like Velasquez's dwarf she was a social outcast. Then one summer, to the surprise of everyone, Aunt Mehetebel sews a dazzlingly beautiful quilt, which wins first prize at

DOROTHY FISHER

the county fair. Overnight this homely spinster finds herself transformed from outcast into artist, a valued individual who shares "in the human dignity of the instinct to create." On first reading, "The Bedquilt" could easily be dismissed as a nice homely story about a Yankee spinster, but dig a little deeper and you discover a forceful message about society's contempt for women's work, especially their work within the home.

Dorothy Canfield Fisher was a household name to fiction lovers in the first half of the twentieth century. The author of bestselling novels and stories, by the 1920s she was an admired writer in what was still at that time a male-dominated profession. While Fisher always thought of herself as a Vermonter, she was actually born in Lawrence, Kansas, where her father was a professor of political economy and sociology. James Hulme Canfield, a crusading educator, had spent much of his career moving his family from one university town to another. But the Canfields also had deep roots in Arlington, Vermont, and James was fond of announcing that he had lived in the Green Mountain State "since 1763."

If Dorothy's father was a traditionalist, her mother, Flavia Camp Canfield, whose roots were also in Vermont, considered herself a free-spirited artist who dismissed tradition as a hindrance to artistic expression, and did not share her husband's love for old-fashioned Vermont values. Dorothy, a traditionalist herself, always felt a close kinship with her father and was often at odds with her impulsive mother. Yet, as a writer of fiction, she owed far more than she was often willing to admit to Flavia Canfield's artistic sensibility.

Even in childhood Dorothy recognized her parents' incompatibility. Lacking the capacity for making each other happy, they both turned to "Dollie," as they called her, for the companionship they could not give one another. This imaginative, quick-witted child accompanied her father to the professional academic meetings her mother detested and, when she was older, joined Flavia on painting and sightseeing trips abroad.

The winters of Dorothy's childhood were passed in various university towns, from Lawrence, Kansas, to New York City. Summers, however, were mostly spent in Arlington, Vermont, with various Canfield great-aunts and uncles in the large brick family house where Dollie had her own little bedroom at the head of the stairs. Her favorite of these elderly relatives was Uncle Zed, a great storyteller. So inseparable were these two that they were dubbed "the Heavenly Twins." When Dorothy was twelve, Zed gave her a Morgan horse.

In 1891, after more than ten years in Kansas, the Canfields moved to Lincoln, Nebraska, where James Canfield spent four years as chancellor of the new state university, and Dorothy completed her high school education. It was in Lincoln that she met the future novelist Willa Cather, then a student at the university. The two became fast friends, and in the winter of 1893–1894, they collaborated on a prize-winning ghost story, "The Fear that Walks by Noonday."

In 1895, James Canfield moved his family to Columbus, where he became president of Ohio State University. Dorothy enrolled there as a student. Shortly after her graduation in the spring of 1899, the family moved even further east, this time to New York City, where Dorothy's father accepted a position as librarian of Columbia University and she began work for a Ph.D. in French literature. Female doctoral students were rare at the turn of the twentieth century, and this lively, petite young woman proved very popular with her fellow graduate students. Her future publisher, Alfred Harcourt, later recalled how lovely she was, "so lovely that we callow youths vied for her favor, entirely unconscious of her extraordinary ability."

Terms at Columbia alternated with terms spent in the libraries of Paris and London. It was on one such visit to Paris with her mother during the 1899–1900 academic year that the two women had traveled to Madrid to see the Velasquez paintings in the Prado. It was a trip that would change Dorothy's life, although she didn't realize it at the time.

Back home in New York, Dorothy continued for the next four years to work toward her doctorate. Before this was completed she received an offer of an assistant professorship from Case Western Reserve University in Ohio to teach French and German. She was delighted by the offer until her parents made it clear they didn't want her living so far from home.

Dorothy complied with their wishes, and once the Ph.D. was in her hands, she found a job as secretary at the experimental Horace Mann School in New York. In her spare time she wrote stories and began selling some of them to magazines. It wasn't long before she realized that she could make a better living writing stories than from her school job, and, without a backward glance, she turned to writing full time.

The next milestone in Dorothy's life came in 1907 when she married a fellow New York writer named John Fisher, who saw through this young woman's urbane social manner to the serious, creative person underneath. After their wedding, Dorothy and John left New York and moved permanently to Arlington. When friends signaled their dismay at this proposed defection from the sophisticated New York literary world, Dorothy responded by voicing her strongly held belief that only in a small town do people really get to know one another. When she published her first collection of stories, *Hillsboro People,* in 1915, the central characters were all based on Arlington neighbors.

The Fishers' marriage was in many respects unconventional for the time. When it became clear that Dorothy's writings were bringing in more money than John's, she was designated chief breadwinner, her husband acting as her principal editor and literary advisor. As early as 1911, Dorothy had earned enough from the publication of her first successful novel, *The Squirrel Cage,* to allow the couple to travel to Rome.

While there, she visited Maria Montessori's experimental school, the Casa dei Bambini. Greatly impressed by its progressive pedagogy, which taught children to be independent, responsible human beings, Dorothy wasted no time in writing about what she had seen. *A Montessori Mother,* was published in 1912 and excited great interest among American parents, who deluged Dorothy with letters asking how the method might be applied to the education of their own children. A year later Dorothy answered these queries with *The Montessori Manual.* Today the American Montessori Society lists some 1,100 member schools, no doubt many of them springing from Fisher's pioneering work in publicizing the Montessori methods. By this time Dorothy was herself a mother, having given birth to a daughter, Sally, in the summer of 1910 and a son Jimmy in 1913.

World War I brought new challenges for the Fisher family. In the spring of 1916 John sailed alone for France to serve with the Automobile Ambulance Service. A few months later, Dorothy, miserable without her husband and ignoring the strong objections of family and friends, crossed the Atlantic with her two children to join him. That winter in Paris proved to be a difficult one for her. John was rarely able to be with her, and seven-year-old Sally came down with a severe case of typhoid. But Sally eventually recovered, and John was appointed supervisor of a training camp for American ambulance drivers, where he put Dorothy in charge of purchasing and preparing food. During their last months in France, Dorothy found charitable work to do on her own, starting a hospital for refugee children and a Braille press for soldiers blinded in battle.

Not until the spring of 1919 did the family return to Arlington, where Dorothy plunged happily back into composing another novel.

Writing fiction, she once said, was "like falling in love." It couldn't be done "by will-power or purpose," but embraced "the *whole* personality." For Dorothy writing fiction also provided a particular kind of satisfaction; it was a way of knowing people and sharing that knowledge with her readers. In a talk she gave at Yale University in 1926, she spoke about two approaches to story writing. One offers its readers an escape from human life. The other, her kind, is an invitation to "reflect more deeply . . . into the significance of human life."

The Brimming Cup is such a work. Published in 1921 by the new firm of Harcourt Brace (whose founder Alfred Harcourt had remained a friend of the Fishers), the novel tells of a marriage and has as its theme the conviction that change takes place inside a person and is not affected by outside circumstances. A best seller, the book was welcomed by readers and reviewers as an antidote to Sinclair Lewis's bleak *Main Street,* also brought out by Harcourt the same year.

Novels and stories, as well as nonfiction, continued to pour from Dorothy's pen. When she wrote fiction she used her maiden name, Dorothy Canfield, but when her nonfiction books, including those she wrote jointly with John, were published, she became Dorothy Canfield Fisher.

By the mid-1920s, Dorothy was sharing a concern, often held by many writers and educators, for deteriorating American reading habits, and wondering how books might be more widely distributed. Then in early 1926 she received an invitation to serve on the selection committee of the newly formed Book-of-the-Month Club. At first Dorothy didn't much like the idea of a committee choosing books that other people should read, nor did she like the name of this new organization. While mulling the subject over, she left home for a few days of shopping in New York.

It was the first warm Saturday of the year, and mid-town Manhattan's streets were jammed with people. Inside Macy's department store Dorothy found the "purchasing mania surged five or six deep" around the linen counter where she wanted to buy some sheets and pillowcases. Fearful that she, a small person, might be crushed, Dorothy made her way back to the street, where conditions were, if anything, worse than when she had entered. To escape the crowds she fought her way onto a double-decker bus. "The seats on its high open roof looked to me as a floating hen house would look to a person swept away by a flood."

Riding the bus uptown, she got off at Brentano's to buy a Spanish dictionary for her daughter Sally. Fighting her way to the door of the bookstore, once inside Dorothy found herself "in a slumberously peaceful atmosphere like that of a remote country churchyard on a sleepy summer afternoon." There was no buying frenzy here. Quite the contrary. Piles of new books lay undisturbed on the counters, and when she was shown up to the mezzanine to find her dictionary, she was the only customer to be seen.

As soon as she was back home in Vermont, Dorothy sat down at her desk and accepted the Book-of-the-Month Club's invitation to serve on its editorial board. For the next twenty-five years she worked tirelessly, helping to choose the books that would be mailed to readers across the country. The work was demanding, if also stimulating. Every month there was a pile of galley proofs of new books to go through, and Dorothy accomplished much of her reading on trains. It was on such a journey that she discovered Pearl S. Buck's *The Good Earth,* all but lost in a collection of manuscripts about Chinese agriculture. At first, this novel, portraying life in rural China, didn't seem that interesting, but before she had read a dozen pages Dorothy found herself unable to put the book down. Her fellow editors agreed it was wonderful. Helped by the publicity of being chosen a Book-of-the-Month selection, *The Good Earth* went on to win the 1932 Pulitzer Prize, and Pearl S. Buck to win the Nobel Prize for literature in 1938.

Increasing demands on Dorothy's time, including her work for the Book-of-the-Month Club, slowed her own writing. Only three of the eleven novels she published were written after she joined that organization. *The Deepening Stream,* her most autobiographical work of fiction, came out in 1930, followed by two more novels, both set in the fictional Vermont town of Clifford. A couple living through a difficult marriage is the focus of *Bonfire,* the earlier of these two novels, but Dorothy herself wrote that for her one of the most important characters in the story "is Vermont, the locality, the valley, the community."

The central figure in the second, *Seasoned Timber,* is a middle-aged school principal, who shares many of Dorothy's father's basic characteristics. Over the course of the story Timothy Hulme, the principal of Clifford's high school, evolves from a proud, even pretentious, old-stock New Englander into a selfless, community-minded educator who, one might say, is Dorothy's ideal Vermonter.

Seasoned Timber was published in 1939 when Dorothy Canfield was sixty years old. It was her eleventh and final novel but by no means her last published work. Stories and other writing continued to come from her pen, including the work she is probably best known for today, *Vermont Tradition: The Biography of an Outlook on Life.* Published in 1953, five years before her death, this highly personal history of the Green Mountain State was, in Fisher's words, intended to show "how Vermont history shaped, molded and created the Vermont character."

After Dorothy Canfield Fisher's death in 1958, her associates on the Book-of-the-Month Club editorial board extolled her as an American of the "rarest and purest character. . . who harked back to and lent new luster to our highest pioneer traditions. A confirmed Vermonter, she was also a cosmopolitan . . . All who knew her felt at once this combination of deep-rootedness and broad humanity; and felt themselves the larger for it."

ELECTRA HAVEMEYER WEBB

1888-1960

Born to Collect

ELECTRA HAVEMEYER WAS NINETEEN YEARS OLD when she first began collecting the American folk art that more than four decades later would find a permanent home in her world-famous museum of Americana in Shelburne, Vermont.

The year was 1908, and Electra was driving through what was then the small village of Stamford, Connecticut, when she noticed the life-size woodcarving of an Indian woman complete with feathered headdress standing just outside a tobacconist's shop. "She spoke to me," Electra later recalled, "I just had to have her." After parking her car, Electra went into the shop and asked the owner if he'd be willing to sell his cigar store Indian, as such figures were then called. "Have you got fifteen dollars?" he inquired, scrutinizing his young customer. Electra admitted to not having enough cash with her, but assured him she could easily get it. So she climbed back into her car and drove home. Having found the money, she persuaded the foreman of Hilltop, the Havemeyers' Connecticut estate, to accompany her back to Stamford in the farm wagon, pick up her new acquisition, and bring it home.

ELECTRA WEBB

Electra never forgot her mother's look of horror when she first laid eyes on the Indian figure. "*What* have you done?" cried Louisine Havemeyer, herself a noted collector of modern painting. Without hesitating, Electra replied that she had bought "a work of art." The older woman started at these words, but refrained from further comment, and the carved Indian woman found a temporary home on the covered porch of another Havemeyer house, this one in Commack, Long Island.

Born in 1888, Electra Havemeyer was the youngest of Henry O. and Louisine Elder Havemeyer's three children. A few years earlier, in 1879, her father, who had inherited his family's sugar business, founded the phenomenally successful American Sugar Refining Company. By the time Electra was six months old, Harry Havemeyer was worth $25,000,000. Less than two decades later, what came to be called his Sugar Trust would be refining more than half of all the sugar produced in the United States.

Despite their great wealth, the Havemeyers were not considered ostentatious, at least not by the extravagant standards of the Gilded Age. Louisine, who presided over the massive Havemeyer mansion on the corner of Fifth Avenue and 66th Street, with its Tiffany interiors and Moorish furniture, was considered frugal by her wealthy friends, and neither she nor her husband showed much interest in the kind of lavish entertaining that rich New Yorkers were used to in the last decades of the nineteenth century. When they were in town, the Havemeyers did hold weekly musicales, opening their house each Sunday afternoon to a select group of friends. Electra later recalled that on those Sundays, following a family lunch in the breakfast room, the Havemeyers' cook would bring up from the kitchen a platter of biscuits, and some paté and cream. The three Havemeyer children, Adaline, Horace, and Electra—appropriately dressed in gingham—under the direction of their mother would mix the paté and cream and spread it on the crackers for the guests to enjoy after the concert, which always began promptly at 3:35 and concluded equally promptly at 5:00.

Collecting art, not entertaining, became the consuming passion of the elder Havemeyers. At the time of their marriage, Harry was happily acquiring old European masters in bulk, but a visit to Paris in the summer of 1895 introduced him to Louisine's great friend, Mary Cassatt. Under the influence of this Philadelphian, who also happened to be an impressionist painter of the first rank, Harry grew to love modern art, and under Cassatt's and Louisine's direction, the couple amassed one of the most notable collections of French impressionism in the United States. As Louisine once explained to an acquaintance in defense of her passion for purchasing art rather than collecting jewels, "I prefer to have something made by a man than to have something made by an oyster."

From the time of Electra's childhood, Louisine had singled her out to carry on the family tradition of art collecting. Unlike her older sister Adaline, who, rather against her will, had been sent to Bryn Mawr College, Electra received an erratic formal education, and was often taken out of school for months at a time to accompany her parents on sightseeing and art-purchasing trips abroad. If the acquisition of the Indian figure in 1908 had dampened Louisine's trust in Electra's artistic taste, her daughter's purchase three years later of a painting by Francisco Goya restored Louisine's faith that her youngest child might yet live up to her high expectations. Electra, however, who possessed a strong sense of self, was determined to show her independence. As far as artistic taste was concerned, she would go her own way.

Electra's formal education, such as it was, did include several years at Miss Spence's School in New York City. Following graduation, on her father's recommendation, she took a business course instead of going to college. Meanwhile, in the fall of 1906 Electra made her social debut. This was followed early in 1907 by the gala wedding of her sister, Adaline, and for a full nine months the whole Havemeyer family found itself caught up in an unprecedented social whirl. No one enjoyed it more than eighteen-year-old Electra. This pretty, petite young heiress, unlike her mother, loved parties and relished giving people a good time.

In July 1905, Electra had gone to Vermont to visit Dr. William Seward Webb and his wife, Lila Vanderbilt Webb, on their four-thousand-acre farm bordering Lake Champlain in Shelburne. She never forgot that first arrival, when she found a coach and four horses waiting to drive her to her hosts. "What an experience that was," she later remembered, "the beauty of Shelburne Farms, Vermont, and Lake Champlain took my breath away." Electra was smitten not only by the loveliness of her surroundings but also with her hosts. "I loved the Webbs, the country, and felt I was in dreamland." It was on this first visit that she was introduced to her future husband, young James Watson Webb, who was four years her senior.

All this gaiety came to an abrupt end for Electra late in 1907, when Harry Havemeyer, worn out by legal battles over his notorious Sugar Trust, died on December 4. Just before his death, he told his youngest daughter, "Boss, take care of your mother." And Electra, who like her father, was always at her best in a crisis, spent the next year and a half devoting herself unsparingly to her mother, who was devastated by the loss of her husband.

Thanks at least in part to Electra's devoted care, Louisine Havemeyer eventually recovered and resumed her collecting in earnest. In the spring of 1909, mother and daughter went abroad for an extended stay, and it was on this trip that Electra made the purchase of the Goya painting so admired by Louisine.

Not long after the two Havemeyer women had returned home they began looking forward to another milestone in their lives. In the last weeks of 1909 Electra became engaged to James Watson Webb, marrying him on February 8, 1910, in St. Bartholemew's on Park Avenue. While the ceremony was described by the *New York Times* as attended by a brilliant assemblage "representative of New York Society," the reception at 1 East 66th Street was an intimate family affair, more to Louisine Havemeyer's liking. Following a honeymoon in Europe, the young couple settled in Chicago, where Watson worked for the New York Central railway, and where their oldest child Electra was born.

By 1912 Watson Webb and his wife returned to New York City, where at first he worked in the telephone industry and later joined the insurance firm of Marsh and McLennan. That first winter was spent with the senior Webbs in their New York apartment. Meanwhile, thanks to a bequest of more than $4,000,000 from her father's estate, Electra and her husband built a lavish house in Syosset, Long Island. It was not a success, however, for both mothers assumed the task of furnishing and decorating to suit their own tastes, placing Moorish chairs in the library and Chippendale furnishings in the dining room. Both Electra and Watson came to dislike the place, and after a few years they bought an old farmhouse in nearby Westbury, which Electra quickly filled with her growing collection of American folk art. Such a declaration of independence on the part of her youngest daughter horrified Louisine Havemeyer, who upon visiting the Westbury house for the first time, cried out, "How can you, Electra, you who have been brought up with Rembrandts and Manets, live with such trash?" Later she would refer to Electra's rustic pieces as "kitchen furniture."

While Electra was decorating her new place in Westbury, she and Watson had also taken possession of a small brick Vermont farmhouse on the senior Webbs' Shelburne estate. The windows had been boarded up when Watson first showed it to his future wife, and to begin with, Electra was not impressed. Under Watson's tutelage, however, she came to love the Brick House, and the couple soon began adding wings to accommodate their growing family and the many friends who visited them. By 1917 the Webbs had four children. A fifth would be born in 1922.

Furnishing these two houses, the one in Westbury and the one in Shelburne, only increased Electra's passion for collecting folk art, a taste that was not shared by many other Americans at the time, including her own offspring. When guests stopped by the Westbury house, which came to include a building housing a tennis court, a swimming pool, and numerous other rooms, her children were likely to say, "Oh, Mother, she's out in the tennis court with her junk." A photograph from the 1940s shows the indoor tennis court, its interior walls lined with folk sculpture, from weather vanes to cigar store Indians. At the same time trunks in the attics of both houses were filling up with every kind of object, from china, pewter, and glass to eagles, dolls, and quilts. Electra herself admitted that this earliest spate of collecting was nothing less than "voracious."

For the next several decades the Watson Webbs divided their time between their Park Avenue apartment, Long Island, and Shelburne. At first they were only able to spend a month each year in Vermont, but later they would take the children out of school for two months, carrying them off to Shelburne, where they themselves enjoyed going foxhunting. Despite these visits, Electra found her time in Shelburne disappointingly short, and more and more was coming to consider Vermont home.

During World War I, while Watson Webb served in the army, Electra, having obtained a chauffeur's license, offered her services as a Red Cross ambulance driver, transporting soldiers returning wounded from France to the city's hospitals. Signing on for night work left her free to be with her children during the day. This work ended with the coming of peace in 1918, and once again she turned her attention to the acquisition of folk art.

It was after her mother's death in 1929, that the idea of housing her collection in a museum first came to Electra. By this time the long rows of trunks in the Brick House were quickly filling up. As Electra pointed out, "Some collectors have the place and look for the piece, not I. I buy the piece and then I find the place." To this need for more space was combined the enthusiastic reception given the Havemeyer family's bequest of more than seventeen hundred objects to the Metropolitan Museum, which made Electra Webb realize that the public might also enjoy her own vast collections.

America's entry into World War II in 1941 disrupted any thoughts she may have had about starting her own museum at that point. Instead, she served as the director of the Pershing Square Civilian Defense Center in New York City. There she oversaw a staff of two hundred volunteers who recruited civil defense workers to serve as firemen, patrolmen, and nurses' aides. Without question, this experience honed Electra Webb's administrative skills, later put to use when she opened her museum.

With the war's end in 1945, Electra returned to the idea of sharing with the public her unmatched collection. As she put it, "I felt I wanted to return to the country the objects that had given me so much pleasure." But she had no idea of where to begin. Her opportunity came in 1947. By this time Electra was fifty-nine, her children had grown, and Watson had retired from his insurance business. Although the Webbs maintained an apartment in New York City, Vermont had become their primary residence.

The Webbs faced another problem: what to do with the collection of carriages that had been ridden in by generations of Webbs and Vanderbilts? Electra had the answer: if the families would contribute the carriages in their possession, she and Watson would buy a piece of property in Shelburne and there erect a suitable building to house and display them to the public.

The family members agreed, and eight acres of land were found with a house, lying just west of the main road through Shelburne. A large horseshoe-shaped barn was erected and quickly filled, both with the family carriages and with wagons, sleighs, coaches, and fire equipment collected over the years by Electra.

Nor did she stop there. By the time the barn was finished, other buildings were taking their places on the eight acres bordering the highway. One of these, an old brick schoolhouse from Vergennes, had been spotted by the Webbs many years earlier on their drives up from New York. Another was a large covered bridge that Electra had rescued from destruction. Where to put it became a big question, since there was no stream on the property for it to cross. Eventually, a pond was dug next to the road where the bridge could cross it and serve as an entrance to the museum.

One day, before the Shelburne Museum was officially opened in 1952, Electra turned to drive into the museum grounds when she saw a car parked in front, blocking the bridge. Although a prominently displayed sign read MUSEUM NOT OPEN. NO ADMITTANCE, a man was standing outside the car taking photographs of his wife. After some time had passed, Electra blew her horn. At this the man turned and asked, "What's the matter? Can't you read?" Electra replied, "Yes, but I work here, and I'm trying to get into the museum to go to work." At which point the man said, "Huh! You work here! You know that Mrs. Webb?" When Electra replied that she did, he retorted, "She must be crazy." Electra asked why he thought so, and was told: "Well, any fool would know that it would have been cheaper to fill up this hole than build this bridge across it!"

Fool or no, Electra Webb opened the Shelburne Museum to the public without fanfare on July 16, 1952. Five buildings were on view, and it took visitors three hours to make the tour.

The next three years proved to be the busiest she had known. In that time, twelve structures were moved to the museum grounds, including several old houses, a lighthouse, and, most spectacular of all, the side-wheeler *Ticonderoga,* a huge 220-foot steel-hulled passenger ship. With its luxurious interiors, complete with wood paneling and gold stenciling, it had plied Lake Champlain since 1906. As with the covered bridge, Electra had rescued the *Ti* from imminent destruction, and for three summers the ship remained on the lake as a floating museum. Then in the winter of 1954–1955, the nearly thousand-ton vessel was transported two miles overland to its present location on the grounds of the museum, an enormously difficult process that by Electra's account "took 62 days of tears."

Back in 1938, on a hunting trip with Watson to Alaska, Electra, a more skilled hunter than her husband, had shot a huge Alaskan brown bear that had been charging their hunting party. While the terrified guide fled, Electra had stood her ground and felled the beast. In the museum's Beach Lodge today there is a photograph of a small Electra, holding a rifle, standing next to a very large brown bear that she had shot—perhaps the one from her Alaska trip. In 1955, as the Webbs were preparing to depart for their last trip to Alaska, one of their sons cautioned Electra: "Please, Mother, if someone offers you Mt. McKinley as a gift for the museum, don't try to move it."

Electra Webb lived for only eight years after her museum opened, but she remained intimately involved with every detail of its operation until the end. When a newly acquired house had to be furnished, she would first search through the many rooms and trunks in the Brick House, and if the perfect article could not be found there, she would buy it or commission someone to make it for her. When it came to the running of the museum, Electra Webb had the last say about everything. She was not only very sure of herself but, as one employee said of her, "She has a way of getting people to do things."

Apart from all the work her museum demanded, Electra Webb also found time to immerse herself in the world of collectors and museum professionals. One of these was her old friend Henry

Francis du Pont, the founder of the Winterthur Museum in Delaware, who would later credit Mrs. Webb with sparking his interest in American antiques.

In these last years Electra also maintained an active social life. This might mean attending a granddaughter's New York debut, or sponsoring a benefit for the Mary Fletcher Hospital in Burlington, where she served as a trustee. In 1956 she was awarded an honorary degree from Yale University, which recognized her for her achievements in the museum field.

Electra Havemeyer Webb turned seventy on August 16, 1958. A description of her at the time conveys:

> a small sturdy woman with a crown of white hair who was always active, but never frantic, she so efficiently organizes her extraordinary flow of energy that she accomplishes an enormous workload which includes running and fussing with her museum, being a devoted grandmother to twelve grandchildren, dashing off to Scotland for a spot of grouse shooting and up to the Adirondacks after deer . . . typing most of her own letters, feeding her Shelburne terriers, running elaborate households in New York and Vermont, and chasing off after a cache of snuffboxes or a rare patchwork quilt.

Two years later, in the autumn of 1960, Electra suffered a stroke while visiting the Trapp Family Lodge in Stowe. For another six weeks she clung to life, not dying until mid-November. By then, however, her work was done, and the great museum that she founded, with its many collections of art and Americana, continues to flourish today, drawing visitors from all over the country and beyond.

HELEN HARTNESS FLANDERS

1890–1972

Green Mountain Ballad Collector

ON AUGUST 10, 1935, the town of Weston was observing Old
Home Day, an annual festival held in communities around the
state, which called on Vermonters who had moved away to return
to their hometowns and spend a day revisiting the scenes of their
youth.

Helen Hartness Flanders, a collector of Vermont folk music,
knew that such gatherings were good hunting grounds for unearthing old ballads. So on that summer day she had driven from her
home in Springfield to the picturesque village of Weston, set deep
in the green hills of the West River Valley. As she drove into
the town center, the sight of the brightly colored balloons and of
people milling about to the lively sound of band music told her she
had come to the right place.

For the past four summers Helen Flanders had been roaming
the state collecting songs and ballads. In most of the towns she visited she knew someone who could introduce her to a likely local
source of folk music, but she knew no such person in Weston. So

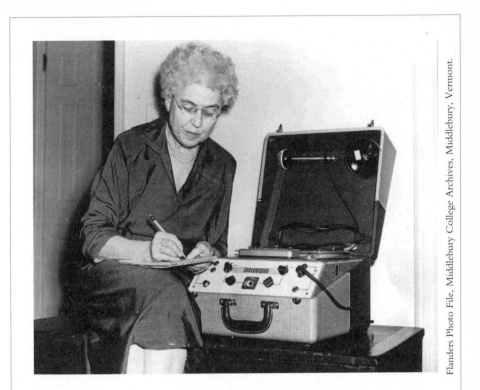

HELEN HARTNESS

this annual celebration, which attracted old timers from far and near, was as good a place as any to start looking.

As she made her way through the festive crowd, Helen caught sight of a genial-looking man leaning against the iron fence that skirted the green. With his "broad white beard, a glinting blue eye and a ruddy complexion," he reminded her of "Santa Claus without his girth." Going up to him, she introduced herself as a stranger in town and asked where dinner was being served. He pointed to the white church up the road. Noting his friendly manner, Helen decided, as she put it, to throw herself upon his mercy. "Maybe you can help me," she began. "I came here hoping I would meet someone who sings very old songs."

"Like, 'I'll chase the Antelope over the Plain,'" came the reply, barely audible over the blare of the band.

"I know only a little," she admitted. "Can you sing more of it?" This was the standard approach ballad collectors used to get people singing, even if the collector herself had never heard of the song. Since the loud band music made it impossible to catch what the man was singing, Helen suggested that they climb into her Ford and drive to the edge of town, which they did. There in his clear expressive voice, this lanky Santa Claus sang all the verses of "Come with Me in My Light Canoe," the first and last of which went like this:

> Come with me in my light canoe
> The sea is calm and the sky is blue
> If we should linger another day
> Storms might rise, and love decay.

> I'll chase the antelope over the plain
> The tiger's cub I'll bind with a chain
> And the wild gazelle with its silvery feet
> I'll give thee for a playmate sweet.

When he had finished, the singer asked Helen if she had ever heard of the ballad "George Holigan." She replied in her usual noncommittal manner, "How does it go?" Without hesitation, he proceeded to sing verse after verse of what she called a "delightful" Irish ballad about a slave ship that turned into a pirate ship on the high seas. When Helen returned home that day she had made a significant addition to her repertoire of folk songs.

Helen Hartness Flanders was born in Springfield, Vermont, on May 19, 1890. Her father, James Hartness, was a self-educated inventor, engineer, and businessman, who would later become president of Jones and Lamson, one of several successful machine-tool companies in Vermont's Connecticut River Valley. From 1921 to 1923 he would serve as governor of Vermont.

Helen, having early shown a talent and an ear for music and languages, spent her high school years at the Dana Hall School in Wellesley, Massachusetts, where she was active in both the glee club and the French club. After graduating in 1909, she returned home to Springfield. From there she made regular trips to Boston to study with Heinrich Gebhard, then the most highly esteemed piano teacher in that city (his most famous pupil would be Leonard Bernstein). If Helen Hartness dreamed of a musical career, those dreams were interrupted, when, a little more than two years after her return home, she married Ralph Flanders.

Ralph, a family friend, had visited Smiley Manse, the Hartness family's home, a number of times during Helen's teenage years. While she had simply dismissed this man as another of her father's business acquaintances, Ralph Flanders had been watching her grow into a young woman with marked interest.

The eldest of a family of nine children, Ralph was born in Barnet, Vermont, in 1879. Although he never attended college, by the early twentieth century he was already making a name for himself as an inventor, and in August 1910 he came to live in Springfield to work for the Fellows Gear Shaper Company. Shortly after his arrival, Ralph became a weekly guest at the Hartness house for Sunday supper. But if he had originally come as a friend of James Hartness, the focus of this young inventor's attention turned to twenty-year-old Helen, a slim dark-haired young woman. As Ralph later wrote in his memoirs, the "realization came to me before it did to her. I finally had to tell her plainly that it was she whom I was visiting."

Soon Helen Hartness and Ralph Flanders were taking long walks in the hills above town every Saturday afternoon, sharing their interest in literature and music. At other times, Ralph enjoyed listening to Helen play the piano. As he later recalled, he never formally proposed to Helen. Instead both came to the gradual realization that they would marry, and on November 1, 1911, the two exchanged vows in the bow window of Smiley Manse.

As Helen later admitted, at first she had difficulty believing that she was actually married to a man who seemed so much older, though in fact Ralph was only eleven years her senior. In her mind he was still her father's friend, "Mr. Flanders," so that she had trouble calling him by his first name. To remedy this, Ralph took Helen to a zoo. There he planted her in front of a cage full of sea lions and they remained there until she had learned from their barking the "correct pronunciation of his Christian name."

For the next twenty years Helen Flanders divided her time between raising three children and playing piano. When arthritis crippled her fingers such that she could no longer play, she turned to organizing a successful community orchestra in Springfield.

Then came an invitation that was to change her life dramatically. In early 1930 Governor John Weeks asked her to join the Committee on Vermont Traditions and Ideals, an arm of the two-year-old Vermont Commission on Country Life. The duties of this committee were to gather for publication a four-volume collection of Vermont prose, poetry, biography, and folklore.

At first Helen was at a loss to understand why she had been asked to join such a group. Her initial impression of its membership, which included such literary lights as Dorothy Canfield Fisher, was that they were "writing folk," mainly interested in preserving Vermont's history, about which she knew little. Only after some persuasion by Arthur Peach, a professor of English at Norwich University and the committee chairman, did she at least agree to attend the first meeting. Peach was certain, he told her, that countless old ballads dating from pioneer times, as well as songs brought to America by earlier generations of settlers, continued to be sung in the Green Mountain State. Though this was a period in which the preservation of folk music was becoming important—Bela Bartok in Hungary, Charles Seeger and John and Allen Lomax in America would be among the movement's leaders—Helen, who had never come across what she called "this hand-me-down singing" herself, was skeptical of its existence. Nonetheless, at this first meeting of the committee, she found herself repeating what Peach had told her about all the folk music out there waiting to be collected and made available for Vermonters to enjoy. The next thing she knew she had given herself a job to begin collecting this material. What she didn't know at the time was that this single committee assignment would become her life's work.

Despite her early skepticism, Helen began this assignment by acquainting herself with the literature in the field. She visited nearby libraries, like the one at Dartmouth College. She also sent an open letter to newspapers around the state asking readers if they knew of "any music—old songs or dances specially grown in Vermont?" Meanwhile, she put some of the funding provided by the Commission on Country Life to work by hiring George Brown, a cellist and conductor she had known in connection with Springfield summer orchestra, to help her with her song collecting. For the remainder of that summer, Brown did most of the fieldwork.

At first Helen Flanders spent much of her time at home in Springfield, reading up on folklore and starting a file of the names and addresses of possible contacts. She wrote articles for newspapers inquiring about sources of traditional music. She spoke to friends and neighbors asking if they knew any old songs or ballads. Even school children in the state were encouraged to find out if their parents or grandparents remembered any old songs. As responses to these various inquiries came in, Helen began calling on those singers whose names had been referred to her.

But she was not collecting the words and music of songs and ballads simply to have them filed away on the shelves of some dusty archive. She also wanted to preserve their flavor as live music. To this end she purchased a dictaphone machine—tape recorders didn't appear until the late 1940s—that recorded on both wax cylinders and metal discs and could be run off huge batteries carried with it in the car.

By the end of 1930 Helen and George Brown had collected enough music to fill the volume called *Vermont Folk-Songs and Ballads* published by the Commission on Country Life in 1931. Meanwhile, the state funds allotted for folk song collecting had been spent, and Brown had to be let go, just when Helen herself was becoming aware of the vast quantity of Vermont folk music that was out there ready for her to collect. So she continued the work herself, using her own money for expenses.

After the publication of *Vermont Folk-Songs and Ballads,* Helen received many letters from readers around the country telling her of additional folk music and making her aware of the widespread interest in collecting old songs and ballads. The most important of these correspondents was Phillips Barry, a Harvard musicologist and a leader in the field of folklore. Not only did Barry share with her a collection of Vermont ballads he had secured some years earlier in the town of Newbury, but he became Helen's principal teacher in the technique of fieldwork. At the same time he also enlisted her aid in the pursuit of his chief goal as a ballad collector: to disprove the theory that the oldest narrative songs brought over from England, known as Child ballads, lived on only in the Southern states.

Phillips Barry was soon making yearly visits to Springfield to stay at Smiley Manse, where Ralph and Helen Flanders now lived. Part of this time was spent going over the music Helen had collected. They would also spend a day or two in the field, following up on some leads for new songs that she had saved for his arrival. By 1933, Helen and Barry, to their mutual excitement and delight, had uncovered forty-eight Child ballads in Vermont, tying the number found in Virginia alone. For Helen Flanders, the work of collecting ballads was now an obsession.

The longer she worked in the field, the more she realized the degree to which she and other ballad collectors were in a "desperate race against time." Since the advent of the radio in the 1920s, Americans, entranced by the music they were hearing over the airwaves, had stopped singing traditional songs. And by the 1930s folk singers were a dying breed. Few of the men and women whom Helen Flanders recorded were under the age of sixty. When following up on a lead, she would often knock on a door only to be greeted with the news that "Father has passed away since I wrote you," or "Auntie's memory has failed since her last illness."

In these initial years of ballad collecting, Helen Flanders always cherished the arrival of the first warm days of spring. It "comes to everyone in a different way," she wrote in one of her newspaper articles. "To the folk-song collector . . . spring is far more than a joy in full-running streams and bird songs." Restrained for months by Vermont's terrible road conditions from following up on certain tempting leads "regarding the haunts of especially interesting songs," Helen could think of no greater pleasure than packing her thirty-pound Dictaphone into her open car (not forgetting to pray that someone would help her lift it out), as well as its huge batteries, and blank records. On one such day in 1935, she drove west from Springfield in her "open car, under unshaken buds brown against the high sky," over the hills to see a man recently released from the hospital. His nurse had written Helen to tell her that during the long days of his convalescence, this man had "whiled away many an hour singing all the old songs he could remember." Another springtime venture took her north and east to Rutland where Mrs. Lloyd Wilkins showed her a scrapbook compiled of clippings and several songs transcribed by her mother (born in 1860) "in precise handwriting."

It was right in her hometown, however, that Helen Flanders discovered one of her richest sources. When Ellen M. Sullivan of Springfield, an elderly Irish immigrant confined to her wheelchair, first read *Vermont Folk-Songs and Ballads,* she was not happy with what she found. After informing her daughter that most of the songs "didn't go that way; they weren't right!," the daughter passed on this rather damning criticism to Helen. Instead of being upset, however, the ballad collector was delighted, realizing immediately that this negative appraisal could only mean one thing: Ellen Sullivan knew a lot of folk songs. So Helen wasted no time in calling on her elderly critic. For the remainder of that summer of 1932, many sunny hours were spent on the old woman's front porch, recording song after song onto wax cylinders and discs. What particularly entranced Helen was the ease with which Sullivan passed from Child ballads to songs of Irish rebellions. It was not long before the two women were fast friends.

At this point in her career as a collector, it was clear that Helen had an indispensable asset and this was her easy way with people. Aware how "unnatural" it was "for any New Englander to burst into song for a perfect stranger," she somehow managed to talk her way into the homes of many reticent Vermonters and cajole them into singing for her.

There were occasions, however, when all of Helen's persuasive skills seemed to fail her. In the fall of 1931, she spent an entire day in Tinmouth, a town set high in the hills of southern Rutland County, driving from one remote farm to another following up on folk song leads. When she stopped to ask a man unloading that year's potato crop if he knew the songs every one of his neigh-bors said he did, his response was that he couldn't remember any. Had his memory failed him, she wondered, or was he simply too embarrassed to sing to this strange woman sitting on his doorstep? By mid-afternoon Helen drove out of Tinmouth not having heard a single song. Tired and hungry she stopped at a favorite inn in Wallingford, where after an early supper, she was rewarded for the day's frustrations, as she listened to a "delightful gentleman of 77" sing one old ballad for her after another.

The 1930s were Helen Flanders's busiest years as a collector. Until the end of the decade she worked mostly on her own, confin-ing her efforts to Vermont. Then, sometime before 1940 she met Marguerite Olney, a graduate of the Eastman School of Music in Rochester, New York. Olney was particularly adept at transcribing songs she had heard in the field—a skill Helen had difficulty with. She was also an expert researcher. The two women made many song-collecting trips together. As Helen later remembered, "There are few by roads that do not have some association," few doorways "which, opened by perfect strangers, have not given momentous experiences in texts and tunes."

Meanwhile, the quantity and scope of Helen's collection had grown to such an extent that she decided it was time to give it a permanent home, where it could be properly cared for and made available for use by students of folklore. In May 1941, the Helen Hartness Flanders Ballad Collection was given to Middlebury Col-lege, and Marguerite Olney became its curator. From this time on, additions to the collection were mostly Olney's work, although Helen Flanders always made the initial contact with a prospective singer. At the same time their collecting field was expanding to include folk music from all of New England.

Although Helen continued to collect songs and ballads, by the mid-1940s her husband's burgeoning political career was making inroads on her time. In the summer of 1946, Ralph Flanders was elected to the U.S. Senate. For the next twelve years, whenever Congress was in session, he and Helen spent a good part of each year in the nation's capital.

The high point of Ralph Flanders's Senate career came in the spring of 1954, when he launched a campaign to censure Senator Joseph P. McCarthy for leading an anticommunist witch hunt. The immediate response to Flanders's charge had been outrage, particularly on the part of the Senate Republican leadership. Shunned in the halls of Congress, his fellow Republican senators refused to eat lunch with him. Helen came in each day to keep her husband company in the Senate cafeteria. In the end, McCarthy was duly censured, and when the congressional session ended, Ralph Flanders, who had decided earlier that year not to run for a third term, returned home permanently with Helen to Vermont.

Back home in Springfield she continued to work on her ballad collection. But by this time she was spending less time in the field than Marguerite Olney, due in part to health problems. In 1953 she and Olney had published their first book together, *Ballads Migrant in New England.* A four-volume work followed a decade later, marking the culmination of their joint effort collecting Child ballads. But while *Ancient Ballads Traditionally Sung in New England,* published between 1961 and 1965, listed Helen Flanders as one of the three authors, Olney was not among them. Coincidentally, about this time the two women had a falling out. The exact reasons for this are nowhere made clear, but Olney, who had not only done much of the preparation for publishing as well as the field-work for *Ancient Ballads,* may have felt she had not been properly credited. Equally dispiriting, surely, was Helen's decision in the late 1950s—again for reasons that are not made clear—to stop funding her Ballad Collection at Middlebury College. As this funding paid most of Olney's salary, the college decided to eliminate the position, leaving her without a job. Olney spent the remainder of her life as a recluse, dying when her house caught fire.

By 1960, rather than collecting ballads in the field, Helen was spending most of her time cataloging and writing about the collection she had amassed, still safely housed in fireproof storage at Middlebury College. This now included five thousand pieces of traditional music, obtained from a variety of sources, from farmers and lumberjacks to basket weavers and scissors grinders. There were songs about ancient as well as recent history, ballads about battles and snowstorms and others about love affairs. In the lumber camps, which Helen herself had often visited, the loggers had sung of their daily encounters with danger.

In the end, perhaps the greatest satisfaction Helen Flanders obtained from her ballad collecting was the opportunity it gave her to move outside the privileged and sheltered life she led as the wife of a prominent Vermont businessman and public servant, and to discover a world of people she might otherwise never have known. During their years in Washington, Ralph had once remarked on his "wife's genius for making delightful acquaintances." It was this gift also that made her a successful collector of folk songs, enabling her, as she once put it "to break through" those barriers separating people of differing backgrounds and experience.

Helen Hartness Flanders's last years were passed quietly in Springfield, where she lived until her death in 1972. And if her years of collecting in the field had opened up new worlds for her, they had also left an astounding legacy for future Vermonters, and indeed for all students of folk music. Without Helen's dedication to, and passion for, the work of collecting these songs of the Green Mountain State, a rich oral tradition might well have died away largely unremembered.

CONSUELO NORTHROP BAILEY

1899-1976

Vermont's Own Daughter

CONSUELO NORTHROP WAS NEARLY FIFTEEN, and a sophomore at St. Albans High School, when she first saw the inside of a courtroom. It was September 1914, and the case being tried in the Franklin County Probate Court concerned the will of Francis Houghton, a prominent St. Albans citizen. Houghton had left his wife Emily $225,000—a considerable sum for those days—and several relatives were challenging the will.

The trial's extensive coverage in the press caught the attention of young Consuelo, whose own argumentative skills were being honed as a member of the St. Albans High School debating team. The defendant, Emily Houghton, had once taught Consuelo's younger sister Frederika, which made Consuelo eager to attend the hearings. She later remembered Emily Houghton as "a very small lady" but "bright as a button."

The will in question was hotly contested by three lawyers, who declared openly in court (or at least so Consuelo remembered it) that no woman as *small* as Emily Houghton was capable of handling

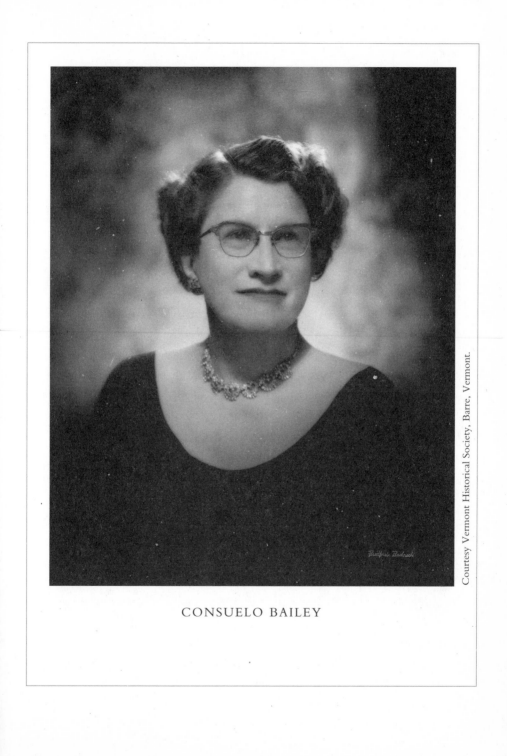

CONSUELO BAILEY

the *large* amount of money involved. To Consuelo, who would go on to become a skilled lawyer and prominent politician, this argument appeared "downright stupid." What had Mrs. Houghton's size to do with the issue at hand? Nothing. Fortunately, the court agreed with her, and Emily Houghton retained her inheritance. Whether or not this first court experience influenced Consuelo's decision to become a lawyer, it surely prompted her lifelong interest in issues of women's equity.

Consuelo Northrop was born on October 10, 1899, in Sheldon Village, a small farming community in northwestern Vermont. Bright, energetic, and fun-loving, this middle child in a family of three girls would always look back with nostalgia to her childhood on the family farm, remembering not only the farm chores but also jumping in the hay, ice skating, and sugar making.

Both Northrop parents believed in giving their three daughters a superior education. Consuelo's mother, a graduate of Johnson Normal School, had been a teacher in Cambridge until she met and married Peter Bent Brigham Northrop, a prosperous farmer. Bent, as he was familiarly known, had always wanted to study law, but had been prevented from doing so for health and financial reasons. Pinning his hopes on his middle daughter, whom he dubbed his "only boy," he encouraged Consuelo to pursue a legal career. Bent Northrop also passed on to his middle daughter an interest in government and a love of Vermont.

While Consuelo's education began in Sheldon, in the fall of 1910 her parents rented a house in St. Albans to take advantage of the schools in this bustling railroad town on the northern shore of Lake Champlain. But each weekend during term time, no matter what the weather, a horse and buggy carried the Northrops ten miles over the rough dirt roads back home to the farm.

A superior high school student, Consuelo had little trouble obtaining a scholarship to the University of Vermont, which she entered in the fall of 1917. The United States was then at war, and she never forgot the cold rented house on Loomis Street in Burlington where she and her mother subsisted that first winter on barley soup.

After graduating Phi Beta Kappa in 1921, Consuelo, who at the time dreamed of pursuing an academic career, took a position in the Shelburne school, where she taught everything from high school Latin and American history, to fourth- and fifth-grade reading. She did not seem to have particularly enjoyed the experience, though she retained her sense of humor sufficiently to report in her memoirs that one of her students had sent her a Valentine containing the verse: "Roses are red, violets are blue, I pity the man who marries you."

The following year, 1922, found Consuelo attending Boston University Law School, where she was one of twenty-five women among one thousand students. For the next three years, she did little else but study at the school she later dubbed "a machine that grinds out lawyers." However, she did find time to join the women's debating team, and was rewarded for her argumentative skills with a membership in the school's honorary debating society. These debating skills would serve Consuelo well in her later career as a politician.

After obtaining her law degree in June 1925, Consuelo returned to Vermont, where she was soon appointed grand juror of the city of Burlington, becoming the first woman to hold this prosecuting office. Some members of the local citizenry, however, found it hard to take her authority seriously. Soon after being sworn in, Consuelo was woken up in the middle of the night by a telephone call from a man who announced, "I want you to come right down here. My wife won't mend my pants!" With some difficulty, Consuelo persuaded the caller that his problem was none of her business.

That October she passed the Vermont bar exam, becoming the seventh female lawyer in the state's history. As grand juror and later as Chittenden County state's attorney—a position she held for four years—she quickly acquired a reputation for being persistent, tough, and uncompromising, especially when it came to dealing with violations of the prohibition amendment. By her account, about twenty search warrants a week were issued from her office. "To the bootlegging community . . . I was always the black beast and the [police] officers often told me that I was promoting more profanity than anyone else for miles around."

If Consuelo succeeded in making her mark in Chittenden County as a successful prosecuting attorney, her true love, she came to realize, was politics. She had enjoyed campaigning for the office of state's attorney, and early in 1930 she decided to run for the state senate, her candidacy being greatly helped by the publicity she had received in the local press. She easily won her seat.

As one of only sixteen women legislators out of well more than two hundred, Consuelo was on trial and she knew it. Stanley Wilson, the governor at the time, apparently believed that a woman's place was in the home. By Consuelo's account, if he didn't exactly want all Vermont's female legislators "assigned to the dishpan . . . [then] I think he would have been more at ease had we all been in the vicinity of the kitchen."

After serving one term in the state senate, during which time she succeeded in winning the respect of Governor Wilson, Consuelo was hooked on politics, and dreaded returning to her law practice. Especially since, as she put it, "The general public did not rush in large numbers to seek the advice of women lawyers." Instead she decided to take a job as executive secretary to Congressman Ernest Gibson and spend some time in the nation's capital. The experience—she remained in Washington from 1931 to 1937—allowed her to immerse herself in the national political scene. She did in fact make many lifelong friends among the nation's political leaders, including Thomas E. Dewey, governor of New York and a leading conservative Republican. Her own growing influence in the party was marked in 1936 when she was chosen to represent Vermont on the Republican National Committee, a position she held for nearly forty years.

By the fall of 1937 Consuelo was back in Burlington practicing law and sharing an apartment with her mother and her younger sister Frederika (her father had died in 1922). Legal clients were few, and Consuelo later said that she occupied her free time reading the Vermont statutes. Then in the summer of 1938 she was hired by a fellow lawyer and political activist, Albon Bailey, to help him with his legal affairs while he ran for the office of attorney general. In the end Albon lost the race but soon gained a wife. He and Consuelo were married on September 11, 1940.

For the next decade Consuelo maintained her law practice, which she shared with Albon until he was forced to retire, having developed Parkinson's disease only months after their wedding. While Albon lived for nearly twenty more years, Consuelo continued to devote her vast energies and ambitions to politics. Frederika made this possible by helping to care for Albon.

In 1944, while attending the Republican National Convention in Chicago, Consuelo Bailey was made a member of the platform committee. Meanwhile, she was much in demand as a speaker and traveled the country giving talks for Republican causes, from supporting Thomas Dewey's presidential candidacy in 1944 to promoting the careers of Republican women in politics.

The high point of Consuelo's own political career came in the 1950s when she succeeded in becoming a Republican Party insider. An old-guard Vermont conservative, Consuelo, as one writer noted, "stayed firmly inside the boundaries of party doctrine when taking public positions." At the same time she was also an active supporter of women's causes, including the Equal Rights Amendment, which she favored long before it became a national issue. One Chittenden County Republican Committeeman remembered the Consuelo Bailey of the 1950s as a very ambitious "political animal" with a wide range of Republican contacts both in and outside Vermont.

Consuelo's most notable political achievement occurred in 1953 when she became the first woman chosen as speaker of the Vermont House. In her election campaign for this highly influential post she visited 225 Vermont towns and 200 of the 246 representatives. Senator George Aiken later told her that he could date his certainty of her victory to a snowy day in December when, after passing her on the wintry highway, he later found her five male opponents "cozily enjoying themselves" in the warmth of a Burlington hotel lobby.

In her acceptance speech on January 7, 1953, Consuelo made a rare public mention of women achieving equality by noting that the first sentence of the first article in the Vermont Constitution claimed that "all men are created equally free and independent" and expressing the hope that "those words will take on a more complete meaning for the women . . . of Vermont." Without question she herself had risen to one of the most powerful positions in the state legislature. As speaker, she had both the right to select committee chairs and the authority to lead the policy debate in the House. But the job was also a particularly challenging one in that it took great skill to harness the conflicting agendas and ideas of a chamber, which before reapportionment in 1965, contained 246 members.

A passage in Consuelo's autobiography, *Leaves Before the Wind,* captures the intense pressure she was often under to keep legislative business moving forward. In one particular instance she asked a house member to move to suspend the rules.

Then unexpectedly, a woman on the south side of the chamber arose and—of all things—moved the House to adjourn! A motion to adjourn is not debatable. The woman by her motion had put me on a spot and a most difficult one. The question was whether or not we would go on with the calendar and put more work behind us. There was also the question whether the House would support the Speaker and her urgent request to advance the legislative calendar. It suddenly flashed through my mind that the moment had arrived when I would definitely know whether during the past months I had acquired what any speaker values above all else—loyalty. That time was now. I had no alternative. I put the question [to the House]. Not one member, not a single solitary member, voted to adjourn. We live a lifetime for a golden moment and for that moment we would give our all. Such was this moment.

Consuelo would later remember her term as speaker as "one of the happiest times of my life." Then on January 7, 1954, exactly one year after she was chosen for this position, she announced that she was running for lieutenant governor, an office that in Vermont usually signaled an ambition for the governorship. The prospect that Vermont might soon have a woman in the state's highest office generated unusual interest in this particular race

During the summer and fall of 1954 Consuelo's campaign style matched that of her run for the speakership, with the important difference that now she was asking the people of Vermont, not just the legislators, to vote for her. In these months before the Republican primary—the only election that counted in this one-party state—Consuelo met people in general stores, gas stations, and churches. She even strengthened her fingers so she could win a milking contest against the other candidates for the lieutenant governorship.

In this particular race she was helped by the fact that she had two men running against her in the primaries. As one newspaper pointed out, a single powerful man might succeed in beating her, but in a race "against more than one male she'll pick up the marbles." This prediction proved correct. Consuelo Bailey won the election in November 1954, and thus became the first woman in the country to serve as lieutenant governor.

But, as she soon discovered, the office of lieutenant governor was considerably less challenging and more ceremonial than that of speaker. As she later wrote: "The year 1955 was one of much speech making at county fairs, dedications of bridges, openings of dog shows." The following August she attended the national convention of the Republican Party as a member of the arrangements committee. Since this convention, which marked the party's centennial, had many women delegates, they played a larger role than usual in the program. Consuelo, for example, was asked to give a speech. This she readily agreed to do until she found herself handed a talk to read. Having never given a prepared speech in her life, and finding the one she was given so "dull witted" that she didn't "wish to be associated with it," she prepared her own written talk, handed it to the teleprompters, and then proceeded to give an entirely different impromptu speech. To her great satisfaction this show of independence was widely reported in the Vermont press.

Consuelo's final act as lieutenant governor was to preside over a joint session of the Vermont legislature on January 10, 1957. Outwardly she did her best to appear, as she later wrote, "carefree and gay," but inwardly "there was a grayness in my heart." She had already announced that she would not seek a second term, thus making it clear that she would not be a future candidate for governor.

She cited her husband's deteriorating health, and indeed, Albon only lived for another two years. But there were other considerations as well, including the belief held by many of her Republican friends and colleagues that Vermonters were not yet ready to elect a woman governor. Not until 1984, with the election of Madeline Kunin, would the state have a female chief executive.

For the remainder of her political life, Consuelo Bailey showed no slackening of interest in public affairs. Setting aside politics at the state level where she had gone as far as she could go, she threw her energies into her role in the Republican Party. In 1964 she was appointed Secretary of the Republican National Committee. She kept that exalted position until 1972, later calling it the high-water mark of her thirty-seven years of work as a committee member. At the 1972 convention in Miami, the last one Consuelo attended, Gerald Ford, who, a year later would become vice-president, introduced her and then handed her his gavel so she could demonstrate that she knew how to use it.

Consuelo Northrop Bailey died four years later, in 1976, at the age of seventy-seven. Her success in achieving high office both in Vermont and in the Republican Party had less to do with proving a woman could do it than with hard work and personal ambition. Consuelo was in many respects a maverick. A consummate politician who drove ahead with the determination of a steam engine, she was not an easy act for other women to follow. And, while she spoke openly of the need for more women in government, she in fact did little to build the kinds of networks with other politically minded women that would have brought more women into the political arena. What she said of Senator Margaret Chase Smith of Maine—who, in 1964, became the first woman in either major party to have her name placed in nomination for the presidency—could equally well have applied to Consuelo herself. As she wrote in her memoirs, *Leaves Before the Wind,* Smith's "achievements were not the result of a Women's Liberation Movement. What she had gained was by her own effort. She had not expected favors because she was a woman," but "had proved, as many other pioneer women had, that nothing is impossible to those who do not count the cost of labor and sacrifice."

SHIRLEY JACKSON

1916-1965

Raising Demons in the Green Mountains

THE IDEA FOR THE STORY CAME TO SHIRLEY JACKSON one fine June morning in 1948. She had been in North Bennington doing her daily errands, and was pushing her daughter Joanne up the long hill home in a stroller filled with the day's mail and groceries, when the germ of a plot began to grow in her mind. Once in the house, she put her baby in the playpen and her vegetables in the refrigerator, and sat down at her typewriter. Shirley later remembered how quickly and easily she had written the story. By the following day, "The Lottery," as she called it, was in the mail to her literary agent.

Shirley's agent didn't particularly like this latest example of her writing, which tells of an annual folk ritual in a small town during which a scapegoat is selected by lottery and then brutally stoned to death by the townspeople. But the agent recognized the story's power and sent it off to *New Yorker* magazine, where several of Jackson's stories had already appeared. The fiction editors, somewhat reluctantly, agreed to buy this one as well. Three weeks later, "The Lottery" came out in the June 26 issue of the magazine, and life was never the same again for its author.

SHIRLEY JACKSON

A week or so after the story's publication, a letter from a friend at the *New Yorker* informed Shirley that her story had "kicked up quite a fuss around the office." When he had heard a man in a bus talking about it, he had wanted to boast about knowing the author, but thought better of it after he listened to what the man was saying. As Shirley later learned, this one story had generated more mail than any other piece of fiction the magazine had ever published.

Up in North Bennington, Shirley considered herself "lucky indeed to be safely in Vermont," where no one in her small town had ever heard of the *New Yorker,* much less read her story. She even became afraid to open her mail, since most of the letters contained negative, even nasty, comments on "The Lottery," including one from her mother urging her "to write something to cheer people up." Timing had a lot to do with this reaction. World War II had just ended, and most Americans were doing their best to forget about evil.

Within a week of the story's publication, the quantity of mail arriving was such that Shirley was forced to change her mailbox to the largest one in the North Bennington post office. From this time on, her name would forever be associated with this single shocking tale, which quickly assumed the status of a horror classic.

Shirley Jackson was thirty-two the year "The Lottery" was published. She and her husband, Stanley Edgar Hyman, who taught at nearby Bennington College, had been living in Vermont for three years. They were the parents of two small children and were expecting a third. The couple had moved up from New York City, but Shirley's roots were in California, where her mother, Geraldine Hardie, was descended from a family of prominent San Francisco architects. Shirley's father, Leslie Jackson, was an English immigrant and a successful businessman.

Born on December 14, 1916, Shirley's early years were spent in the Asbury Park section of San Francisco. Then in 1923, the

Jacksons moved south of the city to Burlingame. Here in this afflu-ent suburb, Shirley went to school, but she also spent hours alone in her room reading and writing poetry. Her one close friend came from a working-class family and was never asked to join the Jack-sons at the dinner table.

By the time Shirley was a senior in high school, the family had moved again, this time to Rochester, New York, then a small, conservative eastern city, which suited Geraldine, but not her unconventional daughter. Here Shirley felt even more out of place than she had in Burlingame.

After a lonely senior year in high school, she enrolled at the University of Rochester. But she fared no better there. Bored by her classes and shunned as an eccentric by her fellow students, by the spring of 1936 she had left the university.

According to her biographer, Judy Oppenheimer, the one place Shirley felt comfortable and powerful was in "the fascinating country of her own mind." So, for a year after leaving the uni-versity, Shirley sat mostly alone in her room at home meeting the goal she set for herself to write a thousand words a day. Then, after this solitary interlude, she decided to apply to Syracuse University, because of its well-respected journalism department. Arriving as a sophomore in the fall of 1937 with every intention of becom-ing a writer, Shirley joined the English instead of the journalism department and began publishing stories in the university's literary magazine. When Stanley Hyman, one of a small vocal group of undergraduates, read one of them, he was so impressed by it that he decided on the spot to make the author his wife, and, filled with possessive bravado, he went to find her.

The young woman he saw could not be called beautiful. Shir-ley never cared much about her appearance. She had always been inclined to pudginess, with fly-away hair, and rumpled clothes. But her bright blue eyes, wide smile, and voice full of laughter revealed a winning zest for life that was immensely appealing. Stanley was smitten.

For her part, Shirley was quickly overwhelmed by Stanley. While she soon learned how difficult and demanding he could be— one friend described him as "the sort of boy everybody's mother hated"—Shirley also recognized his genius and welcomed his pride in both her and her writing. Within a short time the two began living together, and a year after graduation they married, despite loud protests from both families against their union. The Hymans refused to accept a non-Jewish daughter-in-law, and the Jacksons, who harbored a genteel antisemitism, found Stanley a dangerous, boorish radical. The wedding took place on August 13, 1940, in New York City, where the newlyweds lived for most of the next five years.

Married life for the Hymans was both stormy and invigorating from the start. While Stanley quickly found suitable employment, first as an editorial assistant at the *New Republic* and later as a writer for the *New Yorker,* Shirley took longer to get established. At the time of their marriage she had a job selling books in Macy's department store. She quit that after Christmas and went to work for an advertising agency. While Shirley found these jobs intolerably dull, they did provide good subjects for her stories. In the fall of 1941, she and Stanley, taking a break from city life, rented a cabin in New Hampshire for the winter. There Shirley wrote "My Life with R.H. Macy," a story she sold to the *New Republic* for $25. It was her first national publication.

The eldest of the Hymans' four children, Lawrence, known as Laurie, was born in 1942. This was the same year Stanley became a staff writer for the *New Yorker,* and by the following year Shirley too was being published by the magazine, selling the first of twelve stories, "After You, My Dear Alphonse," to them in January 1943.

Despite her growing reputation as a fiction writer, by the mid-1940s Shirley was becoming abnormally sensitive to the dangers of city living. One friend later remembered that even walking down the street seemed dangerous to her; something might fall from a building and kill her. Although these irrational terrors fascinated as much as they paralyzed her, when Stanley was offered a teaching job at Bennington College in southern Vermont, Shirley, pregnant with her second baby and longing to get away from New York, urged him to accept it. By the fall of 1945 the family was settled in a large rented house on one of the main residential streets of North Bennington.

These were good years for Shirley; motherhood and life in the country grounded her and for the next few years her fears and anxieties receded. Some of her short fiction reflected these changes, as rollickingly funny stories about children and about her role as a housewife began appearing in women's magazines the likes of *Good Housekeeping* and the *Ladies Home Journal*. Many of these tales were later collected into *Life Among the Savages,* a cheery book on family life, published in 1953.

But if this new life for Shirley was in many respects both productive and satisfying, to their Vermont neighbors the Hyman household was chaotic at best. Shirley was a doting mother who enjoyed producing hefty home-cooked meals but disliked cleaning. There were cats everywhere and shelves overflowing with books and records. Stanley, who had made it clear from the start that he refused to have anything to do with housework or childcare, spent much of the day either at the college or in his study, a room off-limits to his children. Still, considering the exotic reputation enjoyed by Bennington College—then a little more than a decade old—for liberal ways and bohemian styles, the Hymans were hardly out of character. For the time being at least, their presence was tolerated.

One neighbor later remembered the day he saw a pregnant Shirley struggling up the hill carrying mail, newspapers, and groceries. He was about go over and give her some help when Stanley charged out of the Hymans' house and down the street, presumably intending, the neighbor thought, to help carry his wife's packages. Instead, Stanley carefully extracted the mail from her hands and went back up the street to the house, leaving Shirley, still holding her burdens, to continue trudging home.

In the evenings the Hymans often entertained friends, members of the Bennington faculty and their wives, as well as visiting luminaries in the arts and literature. These lively, alcohol-fueled parties often lasted late into the evening. Stanley may have done most of the talking, but it was Shirley's wit that captivated her guests. When, many people wondered, did she ever find the time to write?

By her children's later accounts, Shirley tried to write every day. During the week, after they left for school, she wrote all morning. When they came home in the afternoon, she was often typing. Even after one of their parents' "legendary parties," the children remembered the sound of their mother's typewriter "pounding away into the night." Friends even recalled one evening when Shirley got up in the middle of a game of Monopoly and went to her typewriter to write a story.

Nineteen-forty-eight was a memorable year for Shirley Jackson. Not only did the appearance of "The Lottery" bring her instant fame, but Farrar Strauss published her first novel, *The Road Through the Wall*. It brought a $500 advance, which, to Shirley's satisfaction, added considerably to the family income. Based on her memories of California, the novel received favorable notice but no wide readership.

Meanwhile, Shirley continued publishing stories in women's magazines, including tales with unmistakably small-town Vermont settings that were not always flattering to the local inhabitants. "The Summer People," for example, describes a city couple who had long spent the months of July and August in a lakeside cottage. One year they decide to stay on after Labor Day. The local people quickly make known their disapproval of this decision. The kerosene man refuses to order more oil for their lamps, the grocery store stops delivering food, and someone tampers with their car. Before many weeks have passed, the summer people get the message and return to the city.

As this tale of calculated persecution reveals, Shirley was capable of seeing the dark underside of life in the kind of small town that others might idealize. She also relished the sinister and the macabre, believing that magic had always been one of her tools. Even her friends readily admitted that Shirley exuded a "powerful aura." Some people said she was a witch.

One story making the rounds of literary circles told of Shirley's anger with the New York publisher Alfred Knopf. Upon learning that Knopf was coming up to Vermont to ski and thus would be within range of her evil eye, Shirley created a wax image of him and broke its leg. Later, when she learned that Knopf, while on the slopes, had not only broken a leg in one place, but in three, Shirley was heard to boast that she had earlier enjoyed similar triumphs with the occult.

In 1951 the Hymans' fourth child and second son, Barry Edgar, was born. The following year Shirley published twelve stories and was finishing *Life Among the Savages,* the first of two popular family chronicles. Appearing in 1953, the novel sold well enough for the Hymans to buy a rambling twenty-room house. With four children to raise, a demanding publishing schedule, and evenings spent with friends, it's hardly surprising that Shirley began to feel the effects of burning the candle at both ends. Blinding headaches and tooth problems led her to try amphetamines and tranquilizers, without cutting back on the amount of alcohol she was known to drink. At the same time she was steadily putting on weight.

In these years Stanley was, as always, Shirley's stabilizer. He may not have been much help with childcare or housekeeping, but his logical, rational mind was a good antidote to Shirley's emotional and unpredictable nature. He steadied her and calmed her in ways no one else could.

Nevertheless, family life became more difficult for Shirley as the children reached adolescence and lost the enchantment that so beguiled her when they were little. Meanwhile, it didn't help that Stanley relished a reputation at the college for being something of a womanizer. He was a popular teacher and welcomed the slavish adoration of his students. But, for a time at least, this reputation had little foundation in fact. Then, shortly after he turned forty, Stanley had a yearlong affair. The knowledge of this, of course, devastated Shirley who had always been made jealous by her husband's flirtatious reputation.

Meanwhile, the Hymans' relations with the North Bennington townsfolk, never comfortable at best, were getting worse. Stanley was disliked for being an atheist and Shirley resented for her depiction of the locals in her fiction, not to mention her occasional irrational outbursts against her children's teachers and other community members who for whatever reason displeased her.

Yet in many ways Shirley was happier in Vermont than anywhere else. There had been a time back in the late 1940s when she and Stanley, feeling isolated by rural life, had tried living in Westport, New York. But the suburbs quickly proved stifling and, after a year or so, they were back in North Bennington. Shirley may not have been particularly friendly with many of the townspeople, but she admired New Englanders, particularly their wry sense of humor and their respect for the privacy she cherished. By the early 1950s, Vermont was home.

When her widely acclaimed ghost story *The Haunting of Hill House* came out in 1959, the *New York Herald-Tribune* called it "a goose pimple horror story, and a good one," and Stephen King would later hail it as "one of the greatest horror novels of all time." Next to "The Lottery," it was the work most readers identified with her name.

While the success of *Hill House* was a triumph for Shirley professionally, it marked the beginning of a long, troubling period at home. The older Hyman children were now adolescents, and while Joanne, a typical teenager preoccupied with her appearance, baffled her mother, Laurie, the oldest began taking advantage of the freedom that his parents allowed him. He did poorly in school and began drinking heavily.

Shirley, meanwhile, was having difficulty writing her next novel. She had a title, *We Have Always Lived in the Castle,* and a subject she had used before: one single personality inhabiting separate bodies. The book's theme was fear, something that until now Shirley had always been able to control. This time, however, she was writing about her own experience of fear in North Bennington. In the novel, the principal characters, two sisters, live alone in a reputedly haunted house at the edge of a village. Whenever one of them goes into town to do an errand, people either deliberately avoid her or taunt her, and sometimes they even throw stones. Shirley claimed in a letter to a friend that such things happened to her every day right in North Bennington. Nothing she had yet written confronted her so directly with her own fears, and, as she progressed with *Castle,* they became so severe she found it difficult to leave the house. Given her past experience with "terrifying" New York, one can't help wondering how much of this fear was within Shirley Jackson and how much really was imparted by her neighbors.

We Have Always Lived in the Castle was published in April 1962. In June, Laurie, aged nineteen, announced that he and his pregnant girlfriend were getting married. Shirley was devastated, certain that her eldest son was throwing his life away. Meanwhile, other factors added to her woes. The last straw was a letter from Geraldine Jackson berating her daughter for her sloppy appearance in a *Time* magazine photo. By Thanksgiving, Shirley could not leave her bedroom and had almost no life at all. Diagnosed with agoraphobia, she also suffered from chronic bronchitis and asthma, while continuing to smoke three packs of cigarettes a day.

For a time psychotherapy helped, but though the agoraphobia itself abated, Shirley found she could no longer write. Not until late in the summer of 1964, after attending the Breadloaf Writer's Conference at Middlebury College with the poet Howard Nemerov—a Bennington faculty member who also suffered from writer's block—did Shirley go back to her typewriter. At first she simply kept a daily journal. Her daughter Joanne, who cared for her that summer, later remembered how her mother "asked the words to free her, and they did." It was not long before she began writing fiction again, beginning work on a new novel, *Come Along with Me,* whose main character was unmistakably herself. By the fall of 1964 she was, by Stanley's account, "a normal human being again."

But Shirley Jackson didn't have much time left to write. On August 8, 1965, she died peacefully in her room of cardiac arrest. She was forty-eight years old. In an obituary published two days later, the *New York Times* noted that "Miss Jackson was at bottom a moralist, who was saying that cruel and lustful conduct is not far below the surface in those who count themselves normal and respectable."

Shirley Jackson hardly fits in neatly with most of the other Vermont women included in this book, particularly with other writers like Dorothy Canfield Fisher and Julia Ripley Dorr, who both tended to idealize Vermont and its small-town life and local ways. Yet this is not to say that she would have been any happier living elsewhere. Her experiences in Rochester, New York City, and suburban Westport show that. And while her best known story, "The Lottery," has sometimes been taken as a parable of the parochialism of narrow, small-town life, Shirley Jackson would probably have written something analogous whether she had lived in New York, or Paris, or some small town in the Midwest.

SELECTED REFERENCES

Lucy Terry Prince

PUBLISHED WORKS:

Gerzina, Gretchen Holbrook. *Mr. and Mrs. Prince: How an Extraordinary Eighteenth-Century Family Moved out of Slavery and into Legend*. New York: Amistad, 2008.

Guyette, E. A. "The Working Lives of African Vermonters in Census and Literature, 1790–1870," *Vermont History* (Spring 1993): 69–84.

Kaplan, Sidney, and Emma Nogrady Kaplan. *The Black Presence in the Era of the American Revolution*. Amherst: University of Massachusetts Press, 1989.

Proper, David R. *Lucy Terry Prince: Singer of History*. Deerfield, Mass.: Historic Deerfield, 1997.

Sheldon, George. "Negro Slavery in Old Deerfield," *New England Magazine* viii, no. 1 (March 1893): 49–60.

UNPUBLISHED SOURCES:

Walker, Mildred. Manuscript of a proposed children's book on Lucy Terry Prince. Courtesy Jane Beck, Vermont State Folklorist.

Ann Story

Fisher, Dorothy Canfield. "Ann Story," in *Four-Square*. New York: Harcourt Brace & Co., 1949.

Hahn, Michael T. *Ann Story: Vermont's Heroine of Independence*. Shelburne, Vt.: New England Press, Inc., 1996.

Hesselgrave, Ruth. "Ann Story," in *Those Indomitable Vermont Women*. Burlington: The Vermont State Division of the American Association of University Women, 2006. 1–2.

Peterson, Max P. *Salisbury from Birth to Bicentennial*. Salisbury, Vt.: The Offset House, 1976.

Thompson, Judge Daniel P. *Green Mountain Boys: A Historical Tale of the Early Settlement of Vermont*. John W. Lovell, 1839.

Weeks, John M. *History of Salisbury*. A.H. Copeland, 1860.

Emma Willard

PUBLISHED WORKS:

Baym, Nina. "Women and the Republic: Emma Willard's Rhetoric of History," *American Quarterly* (March 1991): 1–23.

Brainerd, Ezra. *Emma Willard's Life and Work in Middlebury*. Middlebury, Vt.: Middlebury College, 1918.

Lutz, Alma. *Emma Willard: Pioneer Educator of American Women*. Boston: Beacon Press, 1964.

Scott, Anne Firor. "The Ever Widening Circle: The Diffusion of Feminist Values from the Troy Female Seminary, 1922–1982," *History of Education Quarterly* (Spring, 1979): 3–25.

Willard, Emma. *A Plan for Improving Female Education*. Middlebury, Vt.: Middlebury College, 1918.

UNPUBLISHED SOURCES:

"Emma Willard Scrapbook." Manuscript in Henry Sheldon Museum, Middlebury, Vt.

Clarina Howard Nichols

Blackwell, Marilyn Schultz. "Meddling in Politics: Clarina Howard Nichols and Antebellum Political Culture," *Journal of the Early Republic* 24 (Spring 2004): 27–50.

———. "The Politics of Motherhood: Clarina Howard Nichols and School Suffrage," *New England Quarterly* (December 2005): 570–98.

Eickhoff, Diane. *Revolutionary Heart: The Life of Clarina Howard Nichols and the Pioneering Crusade for Women's Rights*. Kansas City, Kans.: Quindaro Press, 2006.

Gambone, Joseph G., ed. "The Forgotten Feminist of Kansas: The Papers of Clarina I. H. Nichols, 1854–1885," *Kansas Historical Quarterly* (1973–1974).

Kunin, Madeleine May. "Clarina Howard Nichols: Green Mountain Suffragette," *Vermont Life* (Winter 1973): 14–17.

Nichols, Clarina Howard. "Reminiscences," in *History of Woman Suffrage,* Stanton, Anthony and Gage, eds., vol. 1: 178–82. See also in vol. 1: 485–86, vol. 3: 476–77.

Julia Caroline Ripley Dorr

PUBLISHED WORKS:

Dorr, Julia Ripley. "A Book of Remembrance," in Steele, *With Pen or Sword,* ed. Robert G. Steele. New York: Vantage Press, 1979. 2–21.

Hemenway, Abby, ed. *Vermont Historical Gazetteer,* vol. 3, 1101–02, sketch of Julia Caroline Ripley [Dorr] taken from the *Cottage Hearth.*

Leinwohl, Jane, and Elizabeth Ralph. "Julia Caroline Ripley Dorr," in *Those Indomitable Vermont Women.* Burlington: The Vermont State Division of the American Association of University Women, 2006. 18–21.

Steele, Robert G. *With Pen or Sword: Lives and Times of the Remarkable Rutland Ripleys.* New York: Vantage Press, 1979.

UNPUBLISHED SOURCES:

Edwards, Janice Bruso. "A Biographical History of Julia Caroline (Ripley) Dorr." Senior thesis, Green Mountain College, Poultney, Vt., 2000.

Julia Ripley Dorr Papers, Middlebury College Archives, Middlebury, Vt.

Abby Maria Hemenway

Clifford, Deborah. "Abby Hemenway's Road to Rome," *Vermont History* 63 (Fall, 1995): 197–213.

Clifford, Deborah Pickman. *The Passion of Abby Hemenway: Memory, Spirit, and the Making of History.* Barre, Vt.: Vermont Historical Society, 2001.

Hemenway, Abby Maria, ed. *Notes by the Path of the Gazetteer (1886–1889).* Miss Hemenway of the Gazetteer, publisher, Chicago, Ill.

———. *Poets and Poetry of Vermont.* Rutland, Vt.: George A. Tuttle & Co., 1858.

———. *Vermont Historical Gazetteer* (5 vols., 1867–1891).

Morrissey, Brenda. *Abby Hemenway's Vermont: Unique Portrait of a State.* Brattleboro, Vt.: The Stephen Greene Press, 1972.

Rachael Robinson Elmer

PUBLISHED WORKS:

Fish, Frank L. "Rachael Robinson Elmer," *The Vermonter* 24, 1919, nos. 7–8.

Steele, Dorothy. "Rachael Robinson Elmer," *Indomitable Vermont Women.* Burlington, Vt.: The Vermont State Division of the American Association of University Women, 2006.

Steiner, Raymond J. *The Art Students League of New York: A History.* Saugerties, New York: CSS Publications, Inc., 1999.

Straw, Deborah. "Rachael Robinson Elmer and Her New York City Art Post Cards," *Antiques Journal* (October 1997).

Williamson, Jane. "Rowland T. Robinson, Rokeby, and the Underground Railroad in Vermont," *Vermont History* (Winter, 2001): 19–31.

UNPUBLISHED SOURCES:

Elmer, Rachael Robinson. "Diary of a Quaker School Girl," manuscript, Rokeby Museum, Ferrisburgh, Vt.

Some of the books Rachael Robinson Elmer illustrated can be seen at the Rokeby Museum in Ferrisburgh, Vt. Rokeby Museum also has copies of *The Goddard Record* that contain writings by and about Elmer.

For letters to and from Rachael Robinson Elmer, see Rokeby Museum Papers, in the Jessica Swift Research Center, Henry Sheldon Museum, Middlebury Vt.

Dorothy Canfield Fisher

Ehrhardt, Julia C. "Tourists Accommodated with Reservations: Dorothy Canfield's Writings, Vermont Tourism, and the Eugenics Movement in Vermont," in Lois A. Cuddy and Claire M. Roche, eds., *Evolution and Eugenics in American Literature and Culture, 1880–1940.* Lewisburg, Pa.: Bucknell University Press, 2003.

———. *Writers of Conviction: The Personal Politics of Zona Gae, Dorothy Canfield Fisher, Rose Wilder Lane, and Josephine Herbst.* Columbia: University of Missouri Press, 2004.

Fisher, Dorothy Canfield. *A Montessori Mother.* New York: Henry Holt & Co., 1912.

———. *Hillsboro People.* New York: Henry Holt & Co., 1915.

———. *Seasoned Timber.* New York: Harcourt Brace & Co., 1939.

———. *Vermont Tradition: The Biography of an Outlook on Life.* Boston: Little Brown & Co., 1953.

Head, Linda R. "Dorothy Canfield Fisher," in *Those Indomitable Vermont Women* Burlington: The Vermont State Division of the American Association of University Women, 2006.

Madigan, Mark J., ed. *The Bedquilt and Other Stories by Dorothy Canfield Fisher.* Columbia: University of Missouri Press, 1996.

Washington, Ida. *Dorothy Canfield Fisher: A Biography.* Shelburne, Vt.: The New England Press, 1982.

———. "Dorothy Canfield Fisher's *Vermont Tradition,*" in Michael Sherman and Jennie Versteeg, eds., *We Vermonters: Perspectives on the Past.* Montpelier: Vermont Historical Society, 1992. 165–74.

Yates, Elizabeth. *Lady of Vermont.* Brattleboro, Vt.: Stephen Green Press, 1971.

Electra Havemeyer Webb

PUBLISHED WORKS:

Hewes, Lauren B., and Celia Oliver. *To Collect in Earnest: The Life and Work of Electra Havemeyer Webb.* Shelburne, Vt.: Shelburne Museum, 1997.

Joyce, Henry, and Sloane Stephens. *American Folk Art at the Shelburne Museum.* Shelburne, Vt.: 2001.

Saarinen, Aline B. *The Proud Possessors.* New York: Random House, 1958.

Smith, Jean K. "Electra Webb," in *Those Indomitable Vermont Women.* Burlington: The Vermont State Division of the American Association of University Women, 2005. 38–40.

Weitzenhoffer, Frances. *The Havemeyers: Impressionism Comes to America.* New York: Harry N. Abrams, Inc., 1986.

UNPUBLISHED SOURCES:

"Biographical Material—Mrs. J. Watson Webb." Manuscripts in Shelburne Museum Archives, Shelburne, Vt.

Carlisle, Lilian. Transcript of interview by Polly Darnell, May 18, 1999, and May 20, 1999. Shelburne Museum Archives.

Grover, Kathryn. "History of the Shelburne Museum." Manuscript in Shelburne Museum Archives.

Webb, Electra Havemeyer. Notes on "What Started Me with the Museum." Manuscript in Shelburne Museum Archives.

———. "The Shelburne Museum and How It Grew." Talk at Antiques Forum at Colonial Williamsburg, January 30, 1958. Manuscript in Shelburne Museum Archives.

Helen Hartness Flanders

PUBLISHED WORKS:

Brown, Virginia, and Louise Luring. "Helen Hartness Flanders," in *Those Indomitable Vermont Women*. Burlington: The Vermont State Division of the American Association of University Women, 2006. 55–56.

Flanders, Helen Hartness. Articles on collecting ballads in the *Springfield Republican*, 1930–1935. Flanders Ballad Collection, Middlebury College Archives, Middlebury, Vt.

———. "On the Trail of Ballads," *Vermont History* (July 1954): 180–84.

———. "Prospecting for Folk Songs in Vermont," *The Vermonter* (September, 1931): 197–200.

Flanders, Ralph E. *Senator from Vermont*. Boston: Little, Brown & Co., 1961.

Johnson, Sally. "A Legacy of Music: Helen Hartness Flanders Preserved Vermont's Folk Music Traditions," *Vermont Life* (Spring 1991): 1–6.

Post, Jennifer. "The Contributions of Collectors to the Flanders Ballad Collection, 1930–1958," an Introduction to the "Index to Field Recording in the Flanders Ballad Collection," Middlebury College, 1983.

Seigel, Nancy-Jean Ballard. "Helen Hartness Flanders: The Green Mountain Songcatcher," in *Voices, The Journal of New York Folklore* (Fall–Winter 2003).

UNPUBLISHED SOURCES:

Flanders, Helen Hartness. Transcripts of talks and articles in Flanders Ballad Collection, Middlebury College Archives, Middlebury, Vt.:

> "All on a Summer's Day"
>
> "Collectors Luck"
>
> "His Wife Regards Her Senator"
>
> "Meeting 'Fair Charlotte' in Vermont"
>
> "Prospecting for Ballads Traditional in Vermont"
>
> "Prospecting for Folk-Songs"

Consuelo Northrop Bailey

PUBLISHED WORKS:

Bailey, Consuelo Northrop. *Leaves Before the Wind: The Autobiography of Vermont's Own Daughter*. Burlington, Vt.: George Little Press, 1976.

"Consuelo N. Bailey Papers," in *Liber: A Newsletter for the Friends of Special Collections at UVM, University of Vermont* (Spring 1996).

Graffagnino, J. Kevin. "Consuelo Northrop Bailey: Vermont Pathfinder," *Vermont Magazine* (March/April, 2008).

Hand, Samuel B. *The Star That Set: The Vermont Republican Party, 1854-1974.* Lanham, Md.: Lexington Books, 2003.

Taormina, Philene. "Remembering Consuelo Northrop Bailey," *The Vermont Bar Journal* (June 2000): 23–26.

UNPUBLISHED SOURCES:

Madden, Karen Farnham. "Ready to Work: Women in Vermont and Michigan from Suffrage to Republican Party Politics." Ph.D. dissertation, Michigan State University, 2002.

Shirley Jackson

Ames, Carol. "Shirley Hardie Jackson," in *Notable American Women: The Modern Period.* Cambridge, Mass.: Harvard University Press, 1980.

Bain, David. *Whose Woods These Are: A History of the Breadloaf Writers' Conference, 1926–1992.* Hopewell, N.J.: Echo Press, 1993.

Friedman, Lenemaja von Heister. *Shirley Jackson.* Boston: Twayne Publishers, 1975.

Hyman, Stanley Edgar, ed. *The Magic of Shirley Jackson.* New York: Farrar, Straus and Giroux, 1965.

Jackson, Shirley. *The Haunting of Hill House.* New York: Viking Press, 1959.

———. *Life Among the Savages.* New York: Farrar, Straus & Young, 1948.

———. *The Lottery; or, The Adventures of James Harris.* New York: Farrar, Straus & Co., 1949.

———. *Raising Demons.* New York: Farrar, Straus & Co., 1957.

———. *We Have Always Lived in the Castle.* New York: Viking Press, 1962.

Oppenheimer, Judy. *Private Demons: The Life of Shirley Jackson.* New York: G.P. Putnam's Sons, 1988.

ABOUT THE AUTHOR

Deborah Pickman Clifford (1933–2008) lived in Vermont for more than forty years. A graduate of Radcliffe College, she earned her M.A. from the University of Vermont and published three biographies of nineteenth-century American women: Julia Ward Howe, Lydia Maria Child, and Vermont historian Abby Maria Hemenway. In the 1980s she served as the first female president of both the Vermont Historical Society and the Henry Sheldon Museum in Middlebury. She also wrote and lectured widely on the history of Vermont women, twice winning prizes for her articles. In 1995 she was presented with the Governor's Award in Vermont History. Most recently, she and her husband, Nicholas, were joint authors of *The Troubled Roar of the Waters: Vermont in Flood and Recovery, 1927–1931* (University Press of New England, 2007,) a co-winner of the Hathaway Award from the Vermont Historical Society.